Bottle Rush U.S.A.

by Lynn Blumenstein

Author of

"Old Time Bottles"

"Redigging The West"

The story of our historic past
through Old Time Bottles.

PRICE $ 4.25 +

Published by

OLD TIME BOTTLE PUBLISHING COMPANY

Salem, Oregon

ROBERT G. BLUMENSTEIN SR.
Photographer

September
© 1966

COPYRIGHT 1966 BY
OLD TIME BOTTLE PUBLISHING COMPANY

(Cover Picture)

Author and wife trying to persuade their
Burro, Eeyor, to travel the U.S.A.

Printed in the United States of America

Library of Congress Catalog Card No. 66-28187

SBM no. 91.1068 - 02 - 3

ACKNOWLEDGEMENTS

1634772

We wish to express our gratitude to those people who so generously made their collections available for the making of this book.

Harold and Pat Hooper
Vancouver, Washington

Lloyd Mc Mullen
(Obies Restaurant)
Vancouver, Washington

Ted and Hazel Hart
(Harts Antiques)
Vancouver, Washington

Dick Weitzel
Vancouver, Washington

Jules Martinio
Salem, Oregon

E. S. Ritter
(E.S. Ritter Co., Inc.)
Salem, Oregon

Gordon Parson
(Worden Store)
Klamath Falls, Oregon

Murray Wade, Jr.
Portland, Oregon

TABLE OF CONTENTS

PREFACE

It is our endeavor to present to the bottle collector a new and increasing interest that has arisen within the bottle collecting hobby.

Bottle collecting has for many years been in waiting for the new breed of bottle collector, who has recently come upon the scene in such numbers as to alarm the Antique Bottle Collector of preceding years. As in most cases these two groups have joined together to bring bottle collecting to the high place of respect it is enjoying today.

The time and era that bottles represent makes it possible to visualize crude timbered structures, mud streets, rain and sun upon a board walk; a time when man stood solid as a rock, which possibly might become his highest level of manhood. Absent of society's demands of social customs, he lived as he was born, masculine in his own eye's view. He stood proud, firm and progressive, certainly he was not entirely void of custom; however, it was of his own design. Clothed in simplicity, he withstood the elements and was filled with the rawness and lust of his time. He honestly and quickly satisfied his urges and made no excuses. He worked by sweat and blood, without crutches or iron-clad systems to assist or demand for him. Also, this was a time when all big mouths were to be backed up by an equal sized carcass. Because of each days' demand upon him a justification took place. Such were the nights that were filled with a general wildness of rot-gut whiskey and bawdy girls.

The mellowness of his time was the divine stillness of the mornings, each morning chill being subdued by the crackling of sap fir in the wood stove. The air was filled with smells of bisquits, bacon, and ham with potatoes and thick milk gravy in the making. This was truly a time of offering and conquest.

As you move through the proceeding pages of this book, let your mind go and allow yourself to see through pictures, the many stories that are told through bottles.

WALK WITH ME

The trail is long, weary, and often obscure, except for those who have longed for the Big Country and all it holds in the vastness and abundance of the true values of life. The trail may begin in the Adirondacks, through the Appalachians, then on to the Rockies and Sierras, then further north to the Cascades and Bitterroots of Idaho. Walk with me into the wilderness where our lungs ill with the freshness of all things intended for man and woman alike. We shall find a quietness here that shrouds us and forbades the progressiveness of our time. On and on we shall travel, until we find ourselves standing upon a pinnacle. We shall see the sweetness that lingers on a far horizon and feel emotion and wanting. Together we shall realize that surely we must not part from this earth and have contributed nothing more than our own ugly existence.

We part from the main trail and are guided by a path that has been worn deep into the hillside. The path meanders up the rim of a canyon, always keeping to the ridges for easy travel. The canyon darkens through a dense forest only to break into the open and offer a sky full of desire. We find before us the remnants of some long, lost soul's dream, his old hand hewn cabin and his tunnel gouged out of the earth, boastfully exposing years of man made sweat and blood. Through the rough timbers of his cabin we visualize a life of whiskers, B.V.D.'s and a delightful rawness.

Over the ridges and through the valleys we follow the trail; higher and higher we make our way until we reach the tallest peak where there exists only our God and ourselves. We will stand inwardly naked and uninhibited, and damn the conformity of life.

Where will this trail end? It may never end, for here is where we perceive, who we are and what we are. We will come to realize that here is a greatness that is held out only to those who seek it.

THE NEW BREED

THE DOOR KNOB

A bottle collector spied an old run down house near the center of his home town, the house appeared in terrible condition with its broken down porch, and with ivy working its way through the holes in the windows. The front door stood ajar and inside were piles of rubble. After thinking this an ideal place to search for bottles, the collector walked around the house to the back porch. Under the porch he made several good bottle finds. He removed himself from under the porch and while straightening up noticed a beautiful door knob still attached to the back door. I was more than he could resist. He stepped up on the back porch and proceeded to remove the door knob. It would be added to his other fine specimens, he had collected over the years.

The next day the temptation of the old house brought him back again. To his surprise a lady was sitting on the front porch. He hesitated for a moment in front of the house, then asked the lady rather meekly, "Does anyone live here?" The lady replied, "Why yes, an older gentleman lives in the house." Upon further discussion the bottle collector realized that at the very moment he had removed his prized door knob, the owner of the ramshackled house was eating his dinner in the room just adjacent to the door.

THE NIPPER

After searching the grounds surrounding an old house, an experienced bottle collector sat down to rest a spell. He sat and probed the dirt with a stick, feeling rather discouraged, because he hadn't uncovered any good bottles. When suddenly he noticed a small depression near the back corner of the house. Vigorously he dug in the depression. He uncovered bottle after bottle and when he finished, he counted thirty small brown whiskey hip flasks.

Upon further investigation he learned the owner, who was married to a woman who was a non-drinker and highly opposed to her husband's drinking, had buried these bottles. The collector then concluded, he had stumbled upon this man's long hidden secret.

FOUR GENERATIONS
OF NONDRINKERS

A robust enthusiastic collector approached an old farm house that looked as if it ould be a good hunting ground for bottles. He stepped upon the porch and rang e front door bell. A pleasant appearing lady opened the door and inquired as to hat he wanted. Upon looking through the door into the house, he saw that the dy was having tea with several other lady friends. He apologized for intruding d explained that he was a collector in search of old bottles. Also, he would ke to have permission to look around the grounds for liquor bottles. With that xplanation, the lady of the house stiffened up and replied, "If that is what you are ter, you needn't waste your time. As there have been no drinkers in our family in ur generations!" The collector quickly recovered from his blunder and explained at he was interested in other types of bottles also.

After a further discussion concerning the subject, the lady gave him permission explore the grounds. The first place he searched was inside an old outhouse that ood out back. As he lifted a board attached near the outhouse seat, an old em- ossed whiskey bottle became exposed. It appeared that this bottle had been hidden r many years.

THOSE OUTHOUSES

A lady of prominence tells of a digging site where there once had been an old ining encampment. and this site contained long rows of old outhouse pits, and ese pits were now filled with grand old bottles. However, the problem was that e occupants, who lived near by, vigorously objected to anyone digging in that articular area. In fact this collector had been asked to leave the premises four mes by the local sheriff.

On one of her trips she decided to approach the forbidden area by a back way, ping not to draw attention. On her hands and knees she laboriously crawled be- ind various knolls to arrive at the outhouse diggings. Upon arriving at the site, e breathed a sigh of relief and thought to herself, "at last, I have arrived undis- overed and have the place all to myself. Suddenly, three heads popped up like ophers out of various outhouse holes, they shouted in unison, "Quick get into a ole before someone sees you.

She now thinks she has the problem solved for the present. She slips in by the ark of night and quietly digs away by the use of gas lantern.

SERIES COLLECTING

It is interesting to note the many applications that are offered in bottle collecting. Series collecting can be one of intrique and amazement. It is not probable that a person could collect all of the many patent medicine bottles that were placed on the market, but one certainly can advance in that direction, and at the same time keep their collection at a minimum size.

Any type of bottle can be collected in series collecting; however, this discussion is directed toward the patent medicine bottle, as they are more readily available at this time, whether they are purchased or excavated. Generally, this type of bottle can be bought at prices that range from a very few cents to several dollars. In most cases the collector already has many of these bottles in his or her collection at this very moment. It is also understood that as this type of collecting takes hold, the price of these bottles will tend to rise somewhat, as the demand for certain specific types is made. When a whole series is finally completed, the completed set will demand a sharp increase in value, whereas each individual bottle will rise only moderately in value. In series collecting a person may start with the more common types of bottles, such as: Dr. D. Jayne's, Dr. J.H. McLean's, Dr. Kennedy's, Dr. Hiller's, etc., and attempt to collect all of the various styles, types, and sizes that were made by a particular company from its beginning to our present time. This same application also, can be applied to other types of bottles of interest.

JAYNE'S HOUSEHOLD REMEDIES

DR. D. JAYNE'S

FAMILY MEDICINES

Are prepared with great care, expressly for Family Use, and
are so admirably calculated to preserve health and
remove disease, that no family should be
without them. They consist of

Jayne's Expectorant, for Colds, Coughs, Asthma, Consumption,
nd all Pulmonary and Bronchial Affections. It promotes expectoration and
llays inflammation.

Jayne's Tonic Vermifuge, for Worms, Dyspepsia, Piles, General
)ebility, Etc. An excellent Tonic for Children, and a beneficial remedy in
1any of the ailments of the young.

Jayne's Carminative Balsam, for Bowel and Summer Com-
laints, Colics, Cramp, Cholera, Etc. A certain cure for Diarrhœa, Cholera
Morbus, and Inflammation of the Bowels.

Jayne's Alterative, of established efficacy in Purifying the Blood,
nd for curing Scrofula, Goitre, Dropsy, Salt Rheum, Epilepsy, Cancers and
)iseases of the Skin and Bones.

Jayne's Liniment or Counter-Irritant, for Sprains, Bruises,
oreness in the Bones and Muscles, Rheumatism, and useful in all cases where
.n external application is required.

Jayne's Sanative Pills, a valuable Purgative and a certain cure
or all Bilious Affections, Liver Complaints, Costiveness, Dyspepsia, and Sick
Headache.

Jayne's Hair Tonic, for the Preservation, Beauty, Growth and
Restoration of the Hair. A pleasant dressing for the hair, and a useful toilet
rticle.

Jayne's Specific for Tape Worm, a certain, safe and prompt
emedy.

Office of the

Dr. J. H. McLean's Medicine Co

ST. LOUIS, MO.

To the Drug Trade.   Below please find our PRICE LIST:

				Retail at	Per Doz
Dr. J. H. McLean's Strengthening Cordial................ large				$1 00	$7 00
" " " " " .... small				50	3 50
" " " Volcanic Oil Liniment............25 cents size				25	1 65
" " " " " " " ....50 cents size				50	3 30
" " " " " " " .... :$1 00 size				1 00	6 60
" " " Sarsaparilla..................................				1 00	7 50
" " " Vegetable Condition Powders				25	1 25
" " " Chills a d Fever Cure.....................				50	3 00
" " " " " " "				1 00	6 00
" " " Universal Pills				25	1 25
" " " Liquid Vermifuge............................				25	1 25
" " " Candy Vermifuge				25	1 25
" " " Wonderful Healing Plaster,..........(Porous)				25	1 50
" " " Tar Wine Lung Balm.............. ....small				25	1 50
" " " " " " .... medium				50	3 00
" " " " " " .... large				1 00	6 00
" " " Cough and Lung Healing Globules............				25	1 50
" " " Celebrated Catarrh Powder...................				50	3 50
" " " Liver and Kidney Balm.......................				1.00	7 50
" " " " " " Pillets				25	1 50
" " " Strengthening Eye Salve.....................				25	1 50

ALMANACS FOR 1889.

The Thirty-sixth Annual Issue of Dr. J. H. McLEAN'S MEDICAL ALMANAC, published in English, German, French, Swedish, Norwegian, Bohemian, Spanish, Holland-ish, is now ready for distribution. Among the many attractive features of Dr. J. H. McLEAN'S MEDICAL ALMANAC for 1889, are:

THE LAND OF LITTLE PEOPLE, profusely illustrated.

STORM CALLENDAR, for the year 1889, by the Rev. Irl R. Hicks, "THE STORM PROPHET," indicating at a glance the days on which storms may be expected.

Send us a Two Cent Stamp for Sample Copy.

You can Order Almancs from LANGLEY & MICHAELS CO.

SAN FRANCISCO, CAL.

Respectfully Your Friends,

THE DR. J. H. McLEAN MEDICINE CO.

Donald Kennedy's Medicines

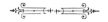

MEDICAL DISCOVERY, warranted to cure every kind of humor, from a common Pimple to the worst kind of Scrofula, Cancer excepted. Price $1.50.

PRAIRIE WEED, a Balsam and Tonic for the cure of **Coughs, Colds, Inflammation of the Throat and Lungs,** and all difficulties tending to **Consumption.**
Price $1.00.

RHEUMATIC AND NEURALGIA DISSOLVENT will neutralize and dissolve the virus that causes **Neuralgia, Sciatica, Lumbago,** and all Rheumatic Pains in any part of the system. Price $1.50.

RHEUMATIC LINIMENT. The best outward application for **Pains, Bruises and Aches** of all kinds.
Price 50 cts.

SALT-RHEUM OINTMENT cures all **Inflammatory Skin Diseases.** Price 50 cts.

SCROFULA OINTMENT. For cleansing and purifying **Scrofulous Sores.** Price $1.00.

HEALING OINTMENT. For cleansing and healing **Ulcers and Old Sores.** Price 50 cts.

SCATTERING LINIMENT. For dissolving and scattering **Strumous Swellings.** Price $1.00.

HAIR GROWER. For **Scald Head and Loss of Hair,** from Dandruff and Heat. Price $1.00.

OR SALE BY ALL DRUGGISTS IN THE UNITED STATES AND CANADA.

No Medicines sent C. O. D., or to be sold on Commission.

WARREN STREET, ROXBURY, MASS.

READ THE LIST!

IT CONTAINS SOMETHING TO FIT EVERY CASE.

CATALOGUE OF Dr. HILLER'S SPECIAL PRESCRIPTIONS

Dr. Hiller's Anti-Bilious Stomach and Liver Cure.
Dr. Hiller's Asthma Cure.
Dr. Hiller's Catarrh Cure.
Dr. Hiller's Cholera Morbus and Cholera Cure.
Dr. Hiller's Cure for Colic and Crying of Infants.
Dr. Hiller's Cure for Sea Sickness.
Dr. Hiller's Cure for Sleeplessness and Nervousness.
Dr. Hiller's Diarrhœa Cure.
Dr. Hiller's Diptheria and Sore Throat Cure.
Dr. Hiller's Dysentery Cure.
Dr. Hiller's Dyspepsia Cure.
Dr. Hiller's Fever Cure.
Dr. Hiller's Headache Cure.
Dr. Hiller's Kidney Cure.
Dr. Hiller's Nervous Debility Cure.
Dr. Hiller's Poison Oak Preventive and Cure.
Dr. Hiller's Pile and Constipation Cure.
Dr. Hiller's Small-Pox Preventive.
Dr. Hiller's Teething Cure.
Dr. Hiller's Whooping Cough Cure.
Dr. Hiller's Worm Cure.
Dr. Hiller's No. 40,*_*_* Cures Painful Menstruation.
Dr. Hiller's No. 50,*_*_* Cures Scanty or Suppressed Menstruation.
Dr. Hiller's No. 60,*_*_* Cures Female Weakness.
Dr. Hiller's No. 70,*_*_* Cures Diseases of the Bladder and Urinary Organs.

Dr. Hiller's Rheumatic and Neuralgic Cure	-	-	$1.00 per Bottle.
Dr. HILLER'S HYDRASTINE RESTORATIVE	-	-	1.00 " "
Dr. Hiller's Cough Cure, small size,	-	-	50 " "
Dr. Hiller's Cough Cure, large size,	-	-	1.00 " "
Abyssinian Desert Companion,	-	-	1.00 " "

*_*_* Nos. 40, 50, 60 and 70 may be ordered by name or number.

NOTE —With the exception of Hiller's Hydrastine Restorative, Dr. Hiller's Rheumatic and Neuralg
Cure, and Dr. Hiller's Cough Cure, the above remedies are put up in Tablet form.
None genuine without the signature of the **Hiller Drug Company**, any imitation of which will be pros
cuted as forgery.   The contents of the bottle are not genuine if the private stamp over the cork and box beari
the *facsimile* signature of The Hiller Drug Co., be broken, tampered with or missing.

Price $1.00 per Box.   Six Boxes for $5.00.

SOLD BY ALL DRUGGISTS.

NOTICE TO THE TRADE.

THE HILLER DRUG CO., has Unequaled Facilities for putting u
Proprietary Medicines.   The Tablets on the List of the Company's Proprietar
Remedies are samples of the Fine Class of work turned out, and for finish the
are unequaled in the world.

Special or Private Formula of Compressed Tablets manufactured to Orde
at Reasonable Rates.

THE HILLER DRUG CO.,

MANUFACTURING CHEMISTS,

LABORATORY, 23 STEVENSON ST.   San Francisco, Cal.

Picture courtesy of Cy and Willetta Kooch (Pioneer Museum, Joseph, Oregon).

EMBOSSING	TYPE	SIZE	COLOR
ight & Taylor stillers uisville, K.Y. 1 Quart gistered	Whiskey	9 1/2	Dark Amber
1 Measure H.	Whiskey	9 1/2	Light Amber
shown	Bullseye	6 1/2	Clear
e A. Colburn Co.	Whiskey (picnic)	4 3/4	Clear

	BOTTOM		
mmodores Royal O.K. d Bourbon, K.Y. rx & Jorgensen rtland, O'GN.	Whiskey	11 3/4	Clear
mbrinus Brewing Co. rtland OR is Bottle is Never Sold	Beverage	11 3/4	Amber
. Harters n Tonic	Tonic	9 1/2	Amber
hann Hoff	Malt Extract	7 1/2	Olive

BOSSING	TYPE	SIZE	COLOR
ade Mark d C.H. Moore urbon & Rye sse Moore & Co. uisville, K.Y. sse Moore-Hunt Co. n Francisco	Whiskey	11 1/2	Amber
J. Van Schuyver Co. Inc. tland, OR.	Whiskey (inside screw threads)	11 1/4	Amber
os. Taylor & Co. le Agents For Vollmer's d Bourbon uisville KY.	Whiskey (whittle effect)	11 3/4	Rich Red Amber
oenix Old Bourbon ber, Alfs & Brune F. Sole AGTS.	Whiskey	11 3/4	Light Amber

BOTTOM

	TYPE	SIZE	COLOR
in bbed Shoulder)	Whiskey	11 1/4	Clear
egon Importing Co. neither rectify compound tland, Ore.	Whiskey	11 1/2	Dark Amber
in bbed shoulder)	Whiskey	11 1/4	Amber
Shown	French Com- memorative (1945)	8 1/2	Light Gold

EMBOSSING	TYPE	SIZE	COLOR
Old Pioneer	Whiskey (pinch bottle)	6 1/2	Clear
Old Thimble Scotch Whiskey Bloch Bros Glasgow	Whiskey	8	Dark Amber
Plain	(pinch bottle)	8	Emerald Green
Plain	(pinch bottle)	8 3/4	Cobalt

BOTTOM

Crown Distilleries Company	Whiskey (inside screw threads)	10	Amber
Copyrighted Old Times Whiskey First Prize World's Fair 1893	Whiskey	10	Clear
Plain	Squat Seal Brandy	10	Clear
Kahn Bros Distillers New York	Whiskey	9 1/2	Clear

EMBOSSING	TYPE	SIZE	COLOR
Congress & Empire Spring Co. Saratoga, N.Y.	Mineral Water	9 1/4	Blue Green
Clark & White New York	Mineral Water	9 1/4	Olive Green
John Gillons & Co. King Wm IV	Liquor	10	Olive Amber
Whyte & Makay Glasgow	Liquor	9 3/4	Aqua

BOTTOM

Plain	Liquor	8 3/4	Olive Green
Plain	Liquor	8 1/2	Jade Green
I. W. Harper	Whiskey	9 1/2	Amber
Roth & Co. San Francisco	Whiskey	10	Amber

MBOSSING	TYPE	SIZE	COLOR
he F. Chevalier Co. :astle Whiskey an Francisco, Cal.	Whiskey (inside screw threads)	11	Amber
lain	Whiskey (whittle effect)	11 3/4	Deep Red Amber
layner Whiskey)istillery roy, Ohio	Whiskey	11 3/8	Dark Amber
lain	Squat Seal Brandy	9 3/8	Amber

BOTTOM

ouis Taussic & Co. an Francisco, Cal.	Whiskey (inside screw threads)	11 1/2	Amethyst
rown Thompson & Co. ouisville, K.Y.	Whiskey	11	Amber Opalescent
lain	Whiskey (3-piece mold)	12 1/4	Olive Gold
lain	Whiskey (3-piece mold)	12	Olive Amber

EMBOSSING	TYPE	SIZE	COLOR
Coca Mariani Paris	Liquor (Whittle effect)	8 3/4	Grass Green
Sandy Mc Donald	Liquor	10	Amber
James Buchanan & Co. LTD. Distillers, By Appointment To His Majesty The King	Liquor	7	Olive
(sig) J. A. Gilka J. A. Gilka Berlin Schitzen STR. No. 9 (crown on bottom)	Liquor	9 1/2	Red Amber

BOTTOM

(label) Gaelic Old Smuggler Scotch Whiskey 1878	Whiskey	8 3/4	Aqua
(no label) Plain	Whiskey	8 3/4	Aqua
Jesse Moore-Hunt Co. Trade Mark San Francisco, Cal. Louisville, K.Y.	Whiskey	11	Amber
Scotts Pure Malt Whiskey	Whiskey	11	Light Amber

EMBOSSING	TYPE	SIZE	COLOR
Brown Forman Co. Louisville KY	Whiskey	11 1/2	Clear
Taylor & Williams Whiskey Louisville, K.Y.	Whiskey	12	Clear
Asparagus Gin The Rothenburg Co.	Gin	10	Aqua
Coblentz & Levy 164 & 166 2nd St. Portland, Oregon	Whiskey	11 1/2	Amethyst

BOTTOM

	TYPE	SIZE	COLOR
HY. H. Lhufeld Co. Premium London Gin	Gin	8	Amethyst
(etched) Gin w/Wreath	Gin	11	Clear
KIA-ORA Trade Mark Reg. Beverages Lemon Orange and Lime made from real fruit juice America O-T LTD, Inc. San Francisco, Calif.	Beverage	11 1/4	Clear
Henry Fleckenstein & Co. Trade Mark	Whiskey	11	Clear

EMBOSSING	TYPE	SIZE	COLOR
(as shown)	Bar Bottle	10 1/4	Clear
(as shown)	Bar Bottle	10 3/4	Clear
Kentucky Dew (enamel lettering)	Bar Bottle	11	Clear
Remington Commercial Co. Distilled Just Right 425 Washington St. Portland, Ore.	Whiskey	12	Clear

BOTTOM

Amer Picon Philippeville	Bitters	11 3/4	Green
Rutherford & Kay	Liquor (3-piece mold)	10 1/2	Olive
White Horse Whiskey	Whiskey (3-piece mold)	10 3/4	Olive
"King George IV" Whiskey Proprietors The Distillers Company LTD.	Whiskey	10 3/4	Olive

EMBOSSING	TYPE	SIZE	COLOR
(etched) Rum w/Wreath	Bar Bottle	10 3/4	Clear
(label) Wild Cherry Juice E. M. Johnson & Co. San Francisco	Brandy	11	Clear
E. L. Bart Dry Gin	Gin	8 3/4	Pale Green
Gordon's Dry Gin London England (wolf on bottom)	Gin	8 3/4	Pale Green

BOTTOM

Neil Doherty Wines & Liquors 176 North St. Boston	Whiskey (union oval- strap side)	9 5/8	Light Amber
Hanley Mercantile Co. San Francisco	Whiskey (inside screw threads- strap side)	10 1/4	Amber
(label) Ye Old Mossroof Bourbon (embossing) RS Roehling I Schutz, Inc. Chicago	Whiskey	9 3/4	Amber
Golden Wedding has had no peers for 50 years Since 1856 Federal Law Forbids Sale or reuse of this bottle	Whiskey	7 3/4	Carnival Glass

EMBOSSING	TYPE	SIZE	COLOR
Plain	Whiskey	9 1/2	Gold Amber
Plain	Whiskey (strap side)	6 3/4	Red Amber
Plain	Whiskey (union oval-strap side)	6 1/4	Gold Amber

1634772

MIDDLE

Plain	Whiskey	7 1/4	Amber Opalescent
Plain	Whiskey (shoofly)	7 5/8	Amber
Plain	Whiskey	7 1/4	Amber Opalescent

BOTTOM

Plain	Whiskey (union oval-strap side)	7 1/2	Gold
Plain	Whiskey (union oval-strap side)	6 3/4	Amber
Plain	Whiskey (union oval)	7 5/8	Gold Amber

EMBOSSING	TYPE	SIZE	COLOR
TOP			
(cobweb design)	Whiskey	8	Clear
Full Pint (cobweb design)	Whiskey	8 1/4	Amber
Plain	Whiskey	8 3/4	Amber
MIDDLE			
Registered Contents 8 oz.	Whiskey	6 1/4	Clear
Union Made Trade Mark	Whiskey (Shoofly)	6	Clear
Union Made Trade Mark	Whiskey (picnic)	6 1/4	Clear
Goldberg Bowen & Co. Wine Merchants San Francisco	Wine (shoofly)	7 1/2	Clear
BOTTOM			
onnie Bros onnie ouisville, KY.	Whiskey (madison)	6 1/2	Clear
lain	Whiskey (picnic)	5 1/2	Amber
abel) udson Brand nitation Extract amaica Ginger	Whiskey (picnic)	4 1/2	Clear

EMBOSSING	TYPE	SIZE	COLOR
Peruvian Bitters	Bitters	9	Amber
Prune Stomach and Liver Bitters The Best Cathartic and Blood Purifier	Bitters	9	Amber
DR Harters Wild Cherry Bitters ST Louis	Bitters	7 1/2	Amber
Plain	Bitters	10 1/8	Amber

BOTTOM

Doyles Hop Bitters 1872 (5 leaf)	Bitters	9 1/2	Amber Opalescent
ST Drakes 1860 Plantation X Bitters Patented 1862 (4 log)	Bitters	10	Gold Amber
Lash's Kidney and Liver Bitters, The Best Cathartic and Blood Purifier	Bitters	9	Clear
Lash's Bitters Natural Tonic Laxative	Bitters	9 1/2	Amber

| | TOP | | |
EMBOSSING	TYPE	SIZE	COLOR
os. Triner hicago	Bitters	10 1/2	Amber
erro China – Bisleri Milano, New York 13/16 PTS.	Bitters	9 3/4	Amber
R. J. Hostetter's tomach Bitters 8 Fluid oz.	Bitters	9	Amber
ash's Bitters	Bitters	9 1/4	Amber

	BOTTOM		
(bottom) J. Walker's VB	Bitters (vinegar)	8 1/2	Aqua Opalescent
(label) Lan & Fox Stomach Bitters	Bitters	8 3/4	Amber
C. W. Abbott & Co. Baltimore	Bitters	10 1/2	Amber
C. W. Abbott & Co. Baltimore	Bitters	8 1/4	Amber
C. W. Abbott & Co. Baltimore	Bitters (sample)	3 1/2	Amber

EMBOSSING	TYPE	SIZE	COLOR
(label) C. K. Wilson's Original Wa-Hoo-Bitters	Bitters	8 3/8	Clear
DR. J. G. B. Siegert & Hijos	Bitters (whit- tle effect & 3-piece mold)	8 1/8	Olive
Plain	Bitters	7 3/4	Amber
(bottom) EJB	Bitters or Tonic	9 1/8	Brown

BOTTOM

Roseburg Brewing Co. Roseburg, OR.	Beer	11 3/4	Brown
(bottom) ARNAS	Beer	8	Amber
"CLA-WOOD" Malt Extract Clarke-Woodard Drug Co. Portland, Oregon	Malt	8 3/8	Amber

EMBOSSING	TYPE	SIZE	COLOR
Independent BR'G. ASS'N Chicago	Beer	11 1/4	Amber
John Wieland's Export Beer S.F.	Beer	7 1/2	Dark Amber
Nebraska Brewing Co. Omaha, Neb	Beer	9	Red Amber
Claussen Brew'g Ass'n Seattle, Wash	Beer (3-piece mold)	9 1/4	Dark Amber

BOTTOM

Barner & Riebe Bottlers Redding, Cal.	Beer	11 1/2	Amber
Etna Brewery Etna Mills	Beer	7 3/4	Amber
Kahny & Burgbacher Bottlers Redding, Cal.	Beer	8	Amber

EMBOSSING	TYPE	SIZE	COLOR
Red Top Ferdinand Westheimer & Sons ST. Joseph, Mo. Cincinnatio, O.	Whiskey	12 1/4	Amber
Claussen-Sweeney Brewing Co. Seattle, Wash.	Beer	12	Green
CB Co. Chattanooga, Tenn.	Beer	11 1/4	Light Amber
AB CO. Albany Brewing Co. Albany, OR.	Beer	11 1/4	Dark Amber

BOTTOM

Dain P Pon Brewing Co. LTD. Honam, Canton (label) Hoi Fook Monastery Honam, Canton	Beer (re-bottled with mineral water)	11 1/4	Olive Amber
As Shown	Beer (re-bottled with mineral water)	11 1/4	Gold Amber
label as shown above	Beer (re-bottled with Mineral water)	11	Green
Sakura Beer	Beer	11	Amber

TOP

MBOSSING	TYPE	SIZE	COLOR
lain	Beer	11 1/2	Amber Opalescent
lain	Beer	11 1/2	Amber Opalescent
lain	Beer	11 3/4	Amber Opalescent

BOTTOM

Plain	Beer	11 1/2	Amber Opalescent
Plain	Beer	11 3/4	Amber Opalescent
Plain	Beer	11 1/2	Amber Opalescent

EMBOSSING	TYPE	SIZE	COLOR
Plain	Ale (3-piece mold)	11	Olive (Black Glass)
Plain	Ale (3-piece mold)	8	Olive (Black Glass)
Plain	Ale (3-piece mold)	10	Olive (Black Glass)

BOTTOM

Plain	Ale (3-piece mold)	9 1/2	Olive (Black Glass)
Plain	Ale (3-piece mold)	8 1/2	Olive (Black Glass)
Plain	Ale (3-piece mold)	9	Olive (Black Glass)

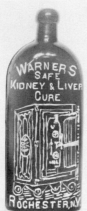

TOP

EMBOSSING	TYPE	SIZE	COLOR
Kola-Cardinette The Palidade M.F.G. Co. Yonkers, N.Y.	unknown	8 3/4	Amber
Warners Safe Kidney & Liver Cure Rochester, N.Y.	Medical	9 1/4	Amber
Johann Hoff	Malt Extract	7 1/2	Green
John Wyeth & Bro Philadelphia Liq. Ext. Malt	Malt Extract	8 3/4	Amber

BOTTOM

Veronica Mineral Water	Mineral Water	10 1/2	Clear
Buffalo Lithia Water Natures Materia Medica Trade Mark	Mineral Water	9 3/4	Aqua
Buffalo Mineral Springs Water, Natures Materia Medica, Trade Mark	Mineral Water (Whittle effect)	10 1/4	Aqua
JNO. Wyeth & BRO.	Cologne (Whittle effect)	11 1/4	Cobalt

EMBOSSING	TYPE	SIZE	COLOR
(label) Abilene Water	Mineral Water	10	Amber
(bottom) Saxlehners Hunyadi Bitterquelle	Mineral Water	9 1/4	Avacado Green
Witter Spring Water net contents 24 oz (bottom) Witter Medical Springs S.F.	Mineral Water	9 1/4	Clear
Witter Springs Water (bottom) W.M.S. Co. San Francisco	Mineral Water	9 1/4	Amber

BOTTOM

Plain	Grape Juice (ten pin)	13	Green
(bottom) Walker's Grape Juice Erie, Pa.	Grape Juice (ten pin)	8 3/4	Clear
(bottom) Erie, Pa.	Grape Juice (ten pin)	8	Olive Green

EMBOSSING	TYPE	SIZE	COLOR
Plain	Gin (case Gin)	10 1/4	Olive
Plain	Gin (case Gin)	9 1/4	Olive
Plain	Gin (case Gin)	6 1/2	Olive

BOTTOM

(Label) Bergomaster Geneva Gin Cobb Hersey Co. Boston	Gin	10 1/2	Olive
Herman Jansen Schiedam	Liquor	8 3/4	Olive
Avan Hoboken & Co. Rotterdam (seal AVH)	Gin	11 1/4	Olive

TOP

EMBOSSING	TYPE	SIZE	COLOR
Plain	Wine (Hocks)	14	Teal Blue
Plain	Wine (Hocks)	14	Amber
Plain	Wine (Hocks)	14	Green

BOTTOM

Garrett's America Wines Garrett & Co. Inc. Established 1835 Virginia Dare Wine New York	Wine	11 3/4	Clear
Plain	Wine	14 1/2	Clear
Plain	Wine (Hocks)	11 1/4	Red Amber

EMBOSSING	TYPE	SIZE	COLOR
Plain	Beverage	9	Aqua
Belfast Ross	Beverage (round bottom)	9 1/4	Aqua
Plain	Beverage (round bottom)	9 1/2	Aqua
Cantrell & Cochrane's Aerated Waters Dublin & Bellfast	Beverage (round bottom)	8 3/4	Aqua

BOTTOM

North Western Brewery Chicago United Breweries Co. This Bottle Not To Be Sold	Beer	9 1/4	Aqua
G. S. Salem, Ore. (Gideon Stolz)	Beverage	7 1/2	Aqua
The Christian Moerlein Brewing Co. Cincinnati, O.	Beer	9 1/2	Aqua
H. Weinhard Portland, OR. bottle is not to be sold	Beer (whittle effect)	7 1/2	Light Green

EMBOSSING	TYPE	SIZE	COLOR
Breig & Shafer	Beverage	6 3/4	Blue Green
J. N. Gerdes S. F. Mineral Water	Mineral Water	7 1/4	Blue Green
Congress & Empire Spring Co. Saratoga, N.Y.	Mineral Water	7 1/2	Olive Green
Johnson Liverpool Trade Mark Registered	Mineral Water (whittle effect— 3-piece mold)	8 3/4	Olive Green

BOTTOM

San Francisco Glass Works	Beverage	7	Aqua
Pioneer Soda Works Trade Mark	Beverage	7 1/4	Blue Green
Pendleton Soda Works	Beverage	6 3/4	Aqua
Corvallis Soda Works	Beverage	8 1/4	Aqua
Corvallis Soda Works	Beverage	8	Aqua

TOP

EMBOSSING	TYPE	SIZE	COLOR
Lawrence & Shaver Georgetown, Wash.	Beverage	8 1/2	Aqua
Trade Mark Vancouver Soda Works Vancouver, Wash.	Beverage	73/4	Light Blue Green
Trade Mark American Soda Works Portland, Ore.	Beverage	71/2	Light Green
Registered The Connecticut Breweries Co. Bridgeport, Conn.	Beer	9 1/2	Light Blue Green

BOTTOM

Registered James Q. Green 2801-07 W. Susquehanna Ave. Philada.	Beverage	11	Clear
(bottom) Hires	Beverage	9	Aqua
Pacific & Puget Sound Bottling Co. Seattle, Wash.	Beverage	81/4	Aqua
Coca Cola Co. Seattle	Beverage	8 1/4	Aqua

EMBOSSING	TYPE	SIZE	COLOR
Cottle Post & Co. Portland OGN	Beverage	7 1/2	Teal Blue
Crystal Spring Bottling Co. Barnet, VT.	Beverage	7 1/8	Clear
JSP (Jas. S. Pederson)	Malt Extract	9	Teal Blue
Plain	Whiskey (union oval – strap side)	6 1/2	Pale Jade Green

BOTTOM

Plain	Medical (Bromo Pop)	7 1/2	Amber
Plain	Beverage	6 1/4	Aqua Opalescent
M. & Co. Martino & Co. 231 Bank St. Wctterbury, Conn. 12 1/2 oz capacity	Beverage	9 1/2	Amethyst
Coca Cola Portland Oregon Trade Mark Registered This bottle never sold.	Beverage	7 1/4	Amber

EMBOSSING	TYPE	SIZE	COLOR
Severa's Febrokura	Medical (for fever)	5 1/4	Amber
Hesperian Curacof	Medical (for colds)	6 1/2	Clear
Nyal's Emulsion of Cod Liver Oil	Medical	9	Amber
Jewel Brand (price 30¢)	Extract (Cloves)	6 1/2	Clear
(label) Perrins Pile Specific The Rock Mountain Pile Remedy	Medical	6	Clear

BOTTOM

(label) LA-CU-PI-A Natures own remedy	Medical (Blood Diseases)	7 3/4	Aqua
(label) Greatest of Tonics Psychine	Medical (consumption)	9 1/2	Aqua
(label) The Celebrated Oregon Kidney Tea The Stark Medicine Co. New York	Medical	8 7/8	Amber
(label) Adler-I-KA Treatment	Medical (for appendicitis)	8	Clear

EMBOSSING	TYPE	SIZE	COLOR
(label) Dr. O. Phelps Brown's Vervain Storative Assimilant	Medical	73/4	Aqua
(label) Dr. O. Phelps Brown's Blood Purifier	Medical	73/4	Aqua
(label) Dr. Shoop's For Scrofula, Syphilis, Sarsaparilla with iron	Medical	7	Aqua
(label) Dr. Shoop's for cure of Rheumatism	Medical	63/4	Aqua

BOTTOM

(label) The specific A NO. 1 a self cure price $3.00	Medical (for the bladder)	5	Aqua
Herbine	Medical	63/4	Aqua
Cooper's New Discovery	Tonic	83/4	Aqua
Nyal's Liniment	Liniment	7	Amber
Herperian Chemical Association	Medical (laxative)	51/2	Aqua

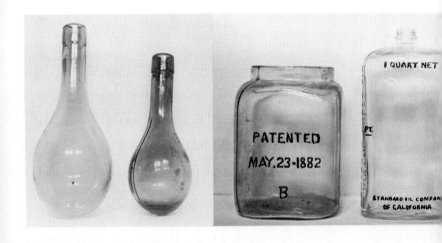

TOP

EMBOSSING	TYPE	SIZE	COLOR
Plain	Medical	8	Cobalt
N.Y. Pharmacal Association	Medical	8 1/2	Cobalt
Plain	Medical	7 3/4	Violet
New York	Medical	9 1/4	Royal Blue

BOTTOM

Plain	Wine	8 1/2	Light Green
Plain	Wine	7	Dark Green
Patented May 23-1882 B	Battery Jar	6	Aqua
Zerolene Valve Oil 1 Quart NET PT Standard Oil Company of California	Oil	7 1/2	Clear

EMBOSSING	TYPE	SIZE	COLOR
Plain (12 panel)	Liniment	7 1/2	Aqua
Plain (12 panel)	Liniment	4 1/4	Aqua
Hostetter's Essence Jamaica Ginger Pittsburg	Extract	6	Aqua
F. B. Browns ESS of Jamaica Ginger	Extract	5 1/4	Aqua
Plain (open pontil)	Ground Cinnamon	6 1/2	Aqua

BOTTOM

ED. Pinaud Paris	Perfume	6 3/4	Clear
Steel & Price Perfumers	Perfume	5 1/4	Clear
Hoyt's German Cologne E. W. Hoyt & Co. Lowell, Mass	Cologne	5 1/2	Clear
Dr. Price's American Perfumes Steel & Price	Perfume	4	Clear
Colgate & Co. Perfumers New York	Perfume	3 5/8	Clear
U-AR-DAS	Cosmetic	2 1/2	Cobalt

EMBOSSING	TYPE	SIZE	COLOR
Dr. J. A. McLean's Tar Wine Balm St. Louis	Medical	7	Light Green Opalescent
Burnett's Coccaine	Medical	6 3/4	Light Green Opalescent
Dr. D. Jayne's Expectorant Philadelphia Half Size Half Dollar	Medical	6 1/4	Light Green Opalescent
R.R.R. Radway & Co. New York ENTD Acord To Act of Congress	Medical	6 1/2	Aqua
Shiloh's Consumption Cure S. C. Well's LeRoy, N. Y.	Medical	6	Blue Green Opalescent

BOTTOM

Plain (flint glass)	Medical	6 5/8	Clear Opalescent
Plain	Condiment	5 1/8	Clear Opalescent
Plain	Medical (3-piece mold)	5 1/2	Clear Opalescent
Plain	Medical (3-piece mold)	4 7/8	Clear Opalescent
Plain	Medical	5	Clear Opalescent

EMBOSSING	TYPE	SIZE	COLOR
Joseph Campbell Preserve Co. Camden, N. J. U.S.A.	Condiment	8 1/4	Clear
Plain (ground top)	Pickle	6 3/4	Clear
Plain (ground top)	Pickle	4 1/4	Clear
Plain	Pickle	4 3/4	Clear

BOTTOM

Plain	Preserve	11	Grass Green
as shown	Liquor	9 1/4	Grass Green
as shown (Fish)	Cod Liver Oil	10	Amber
(label) Cresta Gold	Elixer	11 1/4	Clear

EMBOSSING	TYPE	SIZE	COLOR
Plain	Medical	5 1/8	Aqua Opalescent
Plain	Medical	4 3/8	Clear Opalescent
Plain	Medical	4 1/8	Clear Opalescent
Plain	Medical	4 1/4	Gold Opalescent
Plain	Medical	4 3/4	Amber

BOTTOM

Wyeth & Bro. Philada	Medical (Beef Iron & Wine)	7	Clear
Cuticura System of Blood and Skin Purification Potter Drug & Chemical Corporation Boston, U.S.A.	Medical	7 1/2	Aqua Opalescent
Begg's Hair Renewer	Hair Restorer	7 1/4	Aqua
(label) Mack's Thousand Dollar Spavin Remedy McKallor Drug Co. Binghamton, N.Y.	Medical	6 1/2	Aqua

EMBOSSING	TYPE	SIZE	COLOR
Centaur Liniment	Liniment	5	Aqua
Brownatone Kenton Pharmacal Co. Covington, K.Y.	Medical	4 1/2	Amber
Kendall's Spavin Cure	Medical	5 1/2	Amber
Carbona Carbona Products Co. Carbona	Hair Dressing	6	Aqua
Dr. Drake's German Croup Remedy, The Glessner Med. Co. Findlay, Ohio	Medical	6 1/4	Aqua
Wisdom's Robertine	Cosmetic	4 7/8	Clear

BOTTOM

	TYPE	SIZE	COLOR
Plain	Medical	4 7/8	Aqua Opalescent
Plain	Medical	5	Light Blue
The Owl Drug Co.	Medical	7 1/2	Amethyst
H. Clay Glover Co. New York	Medical	5	Amber
Elys Cream Balm Liquid, Ely Bro's New York	Medical	3 1/8	Cobalt

TOP

EMBOSSING	TYPE	SIZE	COLOR
(label) Gold Medal Quality Hydrogen Peroxide	Household	8	Amber
Trade Mark	Medical	9 3/4	Clear
The Owl Drug Co. San Francisco Chicago, New York, Los Angeles	Medical	9 1/2	Clear
Owl Trade Mark	Medical	7	Clear

BOTTOM

Florida Water Merten Moffitt & Co. San Francisco	Lotion	8 3/4	Light Blue
Balm of a Thousand Flowers Fetridge & Co. New York	Medical (open pontil, very crude)	4 3/4	Aqua
Prepared by Dr. Peter Fahrney & Sons Chicago, ILL. U.S.A.	Medical	5 3/4	Clear
Fellows Syrup of Hypophosphites	Medical	6 3/4	Aqua
Dr. M. M. Fenner's Peoples Remedies Fredonia, N. Y. Kidney & Backache Cure 1872-1898	Medical	8 1/2	Amber

EMBOSSING	TOP TYPE	SIZE	COLOR
Pond's Extract 1846	Medical	9 1/2	Clear
Scott's Emulsion Trade Mark Cod Liver Oil with Lime & Soda	Medical	7 1/2	Blue Green
The Mothers Friend Atlanta, Ga. Bradfield Reg'L Co.	Medical	7 1/4	Aqua
Dr. Shoop's Family Medicines Racine, Wis.	Medical	6 3/4	Aqua

	BOTTOM		
Gambrinus Brewing Co. Portland OR. This bottle never to be sold	Beverage	7 1/2	Amber
(label) Hufeland Original Swiss Stomach Tonic	Tonic	9 1/2	Amber
(label) Alcohol	Brandy	8 1/4	Clear
Plain	Brandy	10	Clear

TOP

EMBOSSING	TYPE	SIZE	COLOR
Ayer's Hair Vigor	Hair Tonic	7 1/4	Peacock
Rumford Chemical Works	Medical	5 3/4	Light Emerald
The Owl Drug Co. Poison	Poison	6 1/2	Cobalt
As shown (Fish)	Cod Liver Oil	6 1/4	Amber

BOTTOM

EMBOSSING	TYPE	SIZE	COLOR
As Shown	Cod Liver Oil	9	Amber
Oregon Blood Purifier WM P Funber & Co. Portland, OR.	Medical	7 1/2	Amber
Frontier Asthma Company Buffalo, N. Y.	Medical	6	Dark Amber
Wakelee's Camelline	Lotion	4 1/2	Amber

EMBOSSING	TYPE	SIZE	COLOR
Dr. Kennedy's Rheumatic Liniment Roxbury, Mass	Liniment	6 5/8	Aqua
Dr. Sanford's New York	Medical (liver invigorator)	7 1/2	Clear
Gargling oil Lockport, N. Y.	Medical	5 5/8	Teal Blue
Hance Brothers & White Philadelphia	Medical (whittle effect)	7 1/8	Amber
Hamilton's Old English Black Oil	Unknown	6 3/4	Aqua

BOTTOM

B. F. Shaw Virginia City, Nev.	Medical	6 1/4	Clear
A. Lernhart Druggist Virginia City, Nev.	Medical	5 1/8	Clear
Franco-American Hygienic Co. Chicago Franco-American Toilet Reguisites	Medical	6	Clear
Forn's Alpenkrauter Blutbeleber Prepared by Dr. Peter Fahrney & Sons Co. Chicago, ILL. U.S.A.	Medical	5 3/8	Clear
Dan'l J. Fry Prescription Druggist Salem, Ogn.	Medical	5 1/4	Light Blue

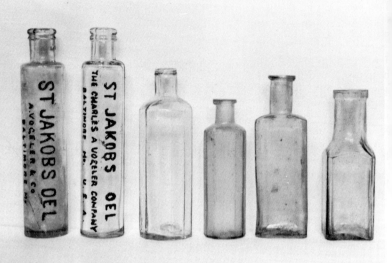

MBOSSING	TYPE	SIZE	COLOR
T Jakobs Oel A. Vogeler & Co. altimore MD.	Liniment	6 1/4	Aqua
T Jakobs Oel he Charles A Vogeler Company Baltimore MD. U.S.A.	Liniment	6 1/4	Aqua
lain open Pontil)	Liniment	5	Aqua
lain	Liniment	4 1/4	Aqua
lain	Medical	5	Aqua Opalescent
lain	Unknown	4 1/2	Aqua Opalescent

BOTTOM

Dr. A. Boshee's German Syrup .M. Green roprietor	Medical	6 3/4	Aqua Opalescent
Dr. D. Jayne's onic Vermifuge hiladelphia	Medical	6 3/4	Aqua
aven Glass hoe Dressing New York U.S.A.	Shoe Dressing	5	Aqua
bericke & Runyon omoeo Pharmacy an Francisco & ortland, OR.	Medical	5 1/8	Clear
he Chas. H. Phillips hemical Co. ew York	Medical	4 5/8	Clear

EMBOSSING	TYPE	SIZE	COLOR
Bartell Drug Stores	Medical	7 3/4	Clear
Citrate Magnesia Sanitas Bottle	Medical	8	Clear
Dr. Hayden's 16 oz.	Medical	7	Light Green
Dr. Sykes Specific Blood Medicine Chicago, ILLS.	Medical	6 1/2	Clear

BOTTOM

Koken Barbers Supply ST. Louis U.S.A.	Hair Tonic	6 3/4	Clear
Heavy Paraffine Oil Gladstone 4 Ounces	Paraffine	5 1/4	Light Green
New Bro's Herpicide Kills the Dandruff Germ	Hair Conditioner	5 3/4	Amethyst
The Owl Drug Co.	Medical	4 1/4	Clear
Sperm Sewing Machine Oil	Oil	4 1/2	Clear
Omega Oil Its Green Trade Mark The Omega Chemical Co. New York	Medical	4 1/4	Clear

EMBOSSING	TYPE	SIZE	COLOR
Knight's Rheumatic Compound, PreP'D by A. P. Knight Chemist, Chicago	Medical	6 1/2	Clear
City Drug Store Dalles, OR	Medical	6	Clear
The N.E. Wilson Co. Inc. Pharmacist Virginia St. Opp. P.O. Phone 425 Reno, Nevada	Medical	5 5/8	Clear
Belt & Son Salem, O'GN	Medical	5 6/8	Clear
Ballard Snow Liniment Co. ST. Louis, MO.	Liniment	4 3/8	Aqua
BOTTOM			
Nathan Tucker MD Specific For Asthma Hay Fever and all Catarrhal Diseases of the Respiratory Organs	Medical	4	Clear
Davis Vegetable Pain Killer	Medical	5	Light Blue
Kickapoo Oil	Medical	5 1/2	Light Blue
Dr. D. Jayne's Expectorant Quarter Size Twenty Five Cents	Medical	5 1/4	Light Blue
The E.E. Sutherland Medicine Co. Paducah, K.Y. Dr. Bell's Pine-Tar-Honey	Medical	5 3/4	Aqua
Espey's Fragrant Cream	Lotion	4 1/2	Clear

TOP

EMBOSSING	TYPE	SIZE	COLOR
abel) ed Seal arkling Ale ickes & Co.	Ale	9 1/4	Olive (black glass)
abel) ude ologne-Veritable C. Boldoot nsterdam	Cologne	9 1/4	Green
ain	Acid	8	Amber
ain	Acid	12	Gold

BOTTOM

EMBOSSING	TYPE	SIZE	COLOR
ain	Beverage	10 3/4	Clear
abel) ineburg's rape Juice	Beverage	12	Green
ouis Bustanoby orbidden Fruit Liquer ederal Law Forbids Sale Re-use of this bottle ne Pint	Liquer	5 1/4	Clear
Pinaud aris	Perfume	10 3/4	Clear

TOP

EMBOSSING	TYPE	SIZE	COLOR
Plain	Unknown	5 1/2	Cobalt
For External use only Prescription Reese Chemo 1000, External use 4 Times daily Mfg. by Reese Chem. Co. Cleveland O.	Medical	5 3/4	Cobalt
(bottom) H. K. Mulford Co. Philadlphia	Medical	5 3/4	Amber
Purola Trade Mark Regd	Complexion Beautifier	5 1/4	Cobalt
Purola Trade Mark Regd.	Cosmetic	6	Blue

BOTTOM

EMBOSSING	TYPE	SIZE	COLOR
Whittemore Boston U.S.A.	Shoe Dressing	5 1/2	Aqua
Creamola Dr. Ward's Medical Co. Winona Minn.	Lotion	5 1/4	Clear
Randall	Beverage	4 1/2	Clear
Welchs Grape Juice	Beverage	5	Clear
Milk of Magnesia Reg. In U.S. Patent Office Aug. 21, 1906 The Chas. H. Phillips Chemical Company Glennbrook, Conn.	Medical	3 1/2	Cobalt

EMBOSSING	TYPE	SIZE	COLOR
Potter Drug & Chemical Corporation Boston U.S.A. Curicura System of Blood and skin Purification	Medical	9	Aqua
Ambler P Keasbey & Mattison Co.	Medical	6	Light Blue
I B Dr. Wistar's Balsam of Wild Cherry Philad A	Medical	5	Aqua
U–AR–DAS for the complection Woodard Clarke & Co. Portland, Oregon	Cosmetic	5 1/8	Cobalt
Dr. D. Jayne's Carminative Balsam Philad A	Medical	5 1/8	Aqua
Bromo Caffeine	Medical	3 1/4	Blue

BOTTOM

Plain	Preserve (whittle effect)	7 1/2	Clear
Plain	Olive	7 1/2	Clear
Plain	Pickle	8 3/4	Light Green Opalescent
Plain	Preserve	6 1/2	Clear
Plain	Preserve	6 1/4	Amethyst

TOP

EMBOSSING	TYPE	SIZE	COLOR
Plain	Preserve	7 1/4	Amethyst
Plain	Preserve	7 1/2	Clear
Plain	Condiment	6 1/2	Amethyst
Plain	Condiment	4	Clear
Plain	Condiment	4 3/4	Amethyst

BOTTOM

EMBOSSING	TYPE	SIZE	COLOR
Grand Union Company ETA Grand Union Tea Co.	Unknown	5	Clear
Grand Union Tea Co.	Unknown	4 3/4	Clear
Vegetable Cosmetic Palmer's Lotion	Cosmetic	4	Clear
A.S. Hinds Co. Portland Maine U.S.A. Hinds Honey and Almond Cream Improves the Complection Alcohol 7%	Cosmetic	2 1/2	Clear
Sharp & Dohme Baltimore	Medical	2 3/4	Amber
Dr. M. Ciesy Druggist Aurora, OGN.	Medical	4 1/4	Clear

TOP

EMBOSSING	TYPE	SIZE	COLOR
Plain	Drug Store	12	Clear
Plain	Apothecary	8 1/2	Clear
Plain	Apothecary	7	Clear

BOTTOM

EMBOSSING	TYPE	SIZE	COLOR
Plain	Candy Jar	9 1/2	Clear
(label) Lewis Packing Co. San Francisco, California	Gherkins	7 3/4	Clear
As Shown	Pottery Jar	6 1/2	Brown & Cream

EMBOSSING	TYPE	SIZE	COLOR
Plain	Preserve	7	Aqua Opalescent
Plain	Condiment	5 1/4	Clear Opalescent
Plain	Condiment	5 1/4	Clear Opalescent
E & C Co.	Condiment	5 1/8	Clear

BOTTOM

Olympic	Preserve	6 1/2	Clear
Horton - Cato M.F.G. Co. Detroit, Mich	Condiment	5 3/8	Clear
Iaccus Bros able Delicacies Wheeling W. Va.	Preserve	5	Amethyst
lain	Catsup	7 1/2	Amethyst
lain	Unknown	3 1/2	Green

EMBOSSING	TYPE	SIZE	COLOR
The Oakland Chemical Company Dioxogen	Chemical	7	Amber
WM Warner & Co. Philadelphia	Medical	7 1/4	Cobalt
Plain	Medical	6	Amber
Plain	Medical	6 1/2	Aqua
The Baradent Co. Inc. San Francisco & New York Creme De Camelia For The Complexion	Cosmetic	5	Cobalt

BOTTOM

EMBOSSING	TYPE	SIZE	COLOR
Wil - low of Boston Incorporated	Unknown	6 3/8	Clear
Baby Brand Trade Mark Castoria	Medical (milk laxative)	6 1/4	Clear
Binz Bronchi-Lyptus	Medical	5 1/2	Amber
Trade Mark Gebhardt Eagle Chili Powder	Condiment	5 3/4	Purple
Tarrant & Co. Druggist New York	Medical	5 1/4	Clear

TOP

EMBOSSING	TYPE	SIZE	COLOR
Plain	Snuff	4 1/4	Amber
Plain	Unknown	4	Cobalt Opalescent
Seabury Pharmacal Laboratories	Pharmaceutical	4	Amber
Eastman Kodak Co. Tested Chemicals Rochester, N.Y.	Chemical	3 1/4	Amber
(bottom) Woodard Clarke & Co.	Cosmetic	4 1/4	Cobalt

BOTTOM

Plain	Cosmetic	6	Cobalt
Plain	Medical	6	Cobalt
Plain	Medical	5 3/4	Cobalt
(bottom) H.K. Mulford Co. Philadelphia	Medical	5 1/2	Cobalt
(bottom) Wyeth Pat.	Medical	5 1/2	Cobalt

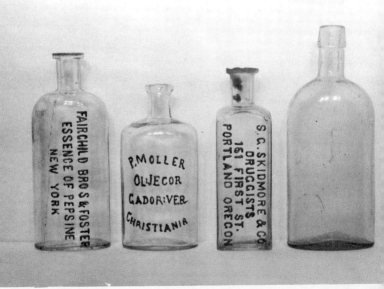

TOP

EMBOSSING	TYPE	SIZE	COLOR
Alfred Wright Perfumer Rochester	Perfume	7 5/8	Clear Opalescent
Solon Palmer's Florida Water New York	Lotion	6 3/8	Aqua
Frederick Stearns & Co. Detroit, Mich. U.S.A.	Medical	4 1/8	Amber
Weeks' Extract for making ginger ale	Extract	4 5/8	Aqua
Bryant's Root Beer This bottle makes five gallons Manufactured by William & Davis Brooks & Co. Detroit, Mich.	Extract	4 1/2	Dark Amber

BOTTOM

EMBOSSING	TYPE	SIZE	COLOR
Fairchild Bros & Foster Essence of Pepsine New York	Medical	7	Clear
P. Maller OL: Jecor Cador: Ver Christiania	Unknown	5 3/4	Clear
S. G. Skidmore & Co. Druggist 151 First St. Portland, Oregon	Medical	6 1/4	Clear
Plain	Amonia	7 3/4	Aqua Opalescent

TOP

EMBOSSING	TYPE	SIZE	COLOR
E.R. Durkee & Co. New York Trade Mark Bottle Patented April 17, 1877	Salad Dressing	8	Clear
Yacht Club Salad Dressing Chicago	Salad Dressing	7 1/2	Clear
Yacht Club Salad Dressing Chicago	Salad Dressing	4 1/4	Clear
Hunt's Pickles	Preserve	6	Clear

BOTTOM

Betsy Brown Safety Nursing Bottle Graduated Scale	Nursing	6 3/4	Amethyst
The Nursing Bottle T.G.W. Co. Millville, N.J. U.S.A.	Nursing	6 1/2	Clear
Plain	Candy Jar	5	Clear

EMBOSSING	TOP		
	TYPE	SIZE	COLOR
Plain	Olive Oil	10	Green
Pure Olive A.E.B.B. Depose France	Olive Oil	10	Aqua
(etched) Jamattet Co. Grasse France	Olive Oil	8 1/4	Clear
as shown	Sauce	6 3/4	Clear
Plain	Capers	6 1/2	Green

	BOTTOM		
Plain	Olive Oil	12 1/2	Aqua
Plain	Olive Oil	8 1/4	Clear
Geo. M. Curtis Pure Olive Oil	Olive Oil	7	Clear
Plain	Olive Oil	7	Clear

EMBOSSING	TOP TYPE	SIZE	COLOR
Red Top Rye Fred. Westheimer & Sons Cincinnati, Ohio ST. Joseph, MO. Louisville, KY	Whiskey (sample)	4 3/8	Amber
Mount Vernon Pure Rye Whiskey Bottled at the Distillery Purity Guaranteed by Hannis Distl'g Co.	Whiskey (sample)	3 1/4	Amber
F. Stearns & Co. Detroit, Mich.	Tonic (sample)	4 1/4	Amber
Plain	Whiskey (sample)	4 1/4	Amber
Plain	Whiskey (sample)	5 1/2	Amethyst
Plain	Whiskey (sample)	4 3/8	Clear
	MIDDLE		
Deep Spring Tennessee Whiskey	Whiskey (sample)	4 3/8	Amber
P. H. Heering	Whiskey (sample)	4 1/8	Clear
Port Inc. Reg.	Whiskey (sample)	4 5/8	Clear
1/10 Pint	Liquor (sample)	4 3/8	Amber
Plain (ribbed shoulder)	Whiskey (sample)	4 3/8	Clear
Plain	Whiskey (sample)	4 1/2	Amber
	BOTTOM		
Plain	Whiskey (sample)	4 3/4	Clear
(bottom) Crown Distilleries Company	Whiskey (sample)	3 1/2	Amethyst
Old Quaker	Whiskey (sample)	3 5/8	Clear
Burnham's Clam Bouillon E.S. Burnham Co. New York	Concentrate	4 1/4	Clear
Fox Clam Tea one fluid oz J. G. Fox & Co.	Concentrate	3 3/4	Clear
Holbrooks & Co.	Sauce	4 5/8	Aqua

EMBOSSING	TOP TYPE	SIZE	COLOR
Plain	Whiskey (sample)	4	Clear
Taylor & Williams Incorporated Whiskey Louisville, KY.	Whiskey (sample)	4 1/2	Clear
Plain	Whiskey (sample)	4 1/4	Dark Brown
CHR. Hansen's Laboratory Little Falls, N.Y.	Medical	2 3/4	Clear
Bullock Ward & Co. Chicago, U.S.A.	Unknown	3 5/8	Clear
Pineoleum	Unknown	3 1/2	Clear
Keith Trade Mark Boston	Unknown	3 1/2	Clear

	MIDDLE		
Plain	Liquor (sample)	5 1/4	Olive
Plain	Liquor (sample)	3 1/4	Amber
Plain	Whiskey (sample)	4	Amber
Plain	Whiskey (sample)	4 5/8	Amber
The Duffy Malt Whiskey Company Rochester, N.Y. U.S.A.	Whiskey (sample)	3 7/8	Amber
Plain	Whiskey (sample)	5 3/8	Amber

	BOTTOM		
Plain (open Pontil)	Perfume	2 5/8	Clear Opalescent
Palmers	Perfume	4 3/4	Emerald Green
Palmers	Perfume	3 1/8	Clear
Palmers	Perfume	3 1/8	Clear
Lubin Parfumeur Paris	Perfume	3 1/8	Clear Opalescent
Plain (ground top)	Bile Pills	2 1/8	Emerald Green
Plain	Perfume	2 1/4	Clear Opalescent

EMBOSSING	TOP TYPE	SIZE	COLOR
Santal DeMidy Paris	Unknown	4	Clear
Imperial Cement	Cement	3	Clear
Major's Cement	Cement	2	Aqua
D.D.D.	Medical	3 1/4	Clear
Caulk's Petroid Cement Improved	Cement	2 1/4	Clear
Caulk's Filling Materials Estb, 1877 Trade Mark ManufD by L. D. Caulk Co. Philada. Pa. one ounce caulk's 20th century alloy	Cement	2	Clear
The Boradent Co. Inc. San Francisco	Unknown	1 1/2	Clear
Cream De Camelia for the Complexion	Cosmetic	2 1/2	Cobalt
MIDDLE			
Hinman Perfumer	Perfume	2 1/2	Clear Opalescent
Plain	Cologne	2 3/4	Clear Opalescent
Plain	Perfume	2	Clear
Hametz Lab.	Pharmaceutic	2 1/4	Amber
Plain	Perfume	2 3/4	Clear Opalescent
Plain	Pill	2 1/2	Clear Opalescent
Mekesson & Robbins	Medical	2	Amber
Cutter	Medical	1 1/4	Dark Amber
BOTTOM			
Plain	Medical (3-piece mold)	5	Clear Opalescent
Plain	Medical (3-piece mold)	5	Amber
Plain	Medical (3-piece mold)	3	Clear Opalescent
Plain (ground top)	Medical (3-piece mold)	2 7/8	Clear Opalescent
Plain	Pharmaceutic	2 1/2	Clear Opalescent
Dr. August Koenigs Hamburger Tropfen	Unknown	3 3/4	Clear
Centaur Liniment	Liniment	3 1/2	Aqua

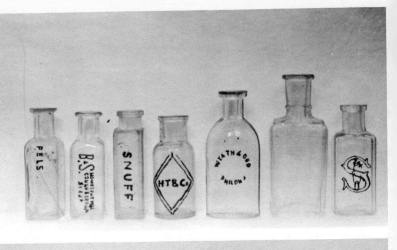

EMBOSSING	TOP TYPE	SIZE	COLOR
Pels	Unknown	3 6/8	Clear
B.S. Homeapathic Cough & Croup Syrup	Medical	3 1/2	Clear
Doct Marshall's Snuff	Snuff	3 1/2	Aqua
H. & T. Co.	Pharmaceutic	3 5/8	Clear
Wyeth & Bro. Phildha	Medical	4	Clear
Sanitol for the teeth	Tooth Powder	4 1/2	Clear
As shown	Unknown	3 1/2	Clear
	MIDDLE		
Creme Simon	Cosmetic	2 1/4	Milk Glass
As Shown	Unknown	2 3/8	Light Green
The Sherwin-Williams Co. Paint & Varnish Makers	Unknown	2 1/2	Clear
Van Stan's Stratena Cement	Cement	2	Aqua
Magnetic Ointment Atrasks	Medical	2 1/2	Aqua
Caulk Detrev's Synthetic Porcelain MFD. by The L. D. Caulk Co.	Cement	1 3/4	Clear
Sharp & Domme Baltimore	Medical	2 1/4	Amber
	BOTTOM		
Kahler Drug Co. the Rexall Store	Medical	3	Clear
Dan'l J. Fry Prescription Druggist Salem O. G. N.	Medical	2 1/2	Clear
Smith Drug Co. Second & James Seattle, Wash.	Medical	2 3/4	Clear
G. O. Guy PH. G. Seattle, Wash.	Medical	3 1/4	Clear
City Drug Store Dalles, OR.	Medical	3 1/2	Clear
A. M. Cole Apothecary Virginia, Nev.	Medical	3 1/4	Clear
T. C. Smith Co. Druggist Salem, OR.	Medical	4	Clear

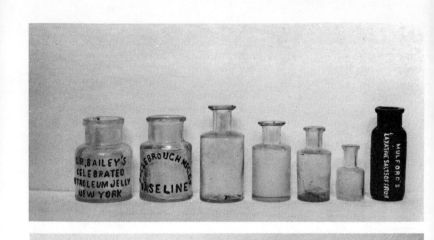

EMBOSSING	TOP TYPE	SIZE	COLOR
C. R. Bailey's Celebrated Petroleum New York	Medical	2 7/8	Clear
Chesebrough MFG Co. Vaseline	Vaseline	2 7/8	Clear
(bottom) Mitchells Centennial Cologne	Cologne	3 3/8	Clear Opalescent
(bottom) Mitchells Centennial Cologne	Cologne	2 3/4	Clear Opalescent
Plain	Perfume	2 1/2	Clear Opalescent
Plain	Perfume	1 3/4	Clear Opalescent
Mulford's Laxative salts of Fruit	Medical	3 1/4	Cobalt
	MIDDLE		
Vanstans Stratena	Cement	2 3/8	Aqua
Plain	Medical	2 3/8	Clear Opalescent
Plain	Medical	2 1/4	Aqua Opalescent
Plain (12 panel)	Medical	2 1/4	Clear Opalescent
Ayers Pills	Medical	2 3/8	Aqua Opalescent
H. W.	Medical	2 1/4	Clear Opalescent
H. W.	Medical	1 3/4	Clear Opalescent
Franco-American Hygienic Co. Chicago	Medical	2 3/4	Clear
As Shown	Perfume	2 1/2	Clear
	BOTTOM		
Plain (frosted neck)	Perfume	2 3/4	Clear
Plain (satin finish)	Unknown	2 3/4	Clear Opalescent
Plain	Unknown	3	Clear Opalescent
Plain	Unknown	3	Amber
Plain	Perfume	2 3/4	Clear
Plain	Medical	3	Clear Opalescent
Eastman Rochester, N.Y.	Chemical	3 1/4	Amber

EMBOSSING	TYPE	SIZE	COLOR
Sanford's Inks and Library Paste	Bulk Ink	9 1/4	Amethyst
Inks (as shown)	Bulk Ink	7 1/4	Amber
Fereous Stone Bottle J. Bourne & Son Patenters Denby Pottere	Bulk Ink	6 1/4	Pottery
Vitreous Stone Bottles J. Bourne & Son Patentees Denby Pottery near Denby P & J Arnold London England	Bulk Ink	7	Pottery

BOTTOM

Carters made in U.S.A. Full Quart	Bulk Ink	9 3/4	Aqua
Plain	Bulk Ink	8	Aqua Opalescent
Sanford's Inks (ground top)	Bulk Ink	5 1/2	Amber

	TOP		
EMBOSSING	TYPE	SIZE	COLOR
Plain (ground top)	Ink	2 1/2	Clear
Sanford's (ground top)	Mucilage	2 1/2	Clear
(bottom) Pauls Pat. Safety Bottle & Ink Co. N.Y.	Ink	2	Clear

	MIDDLE		
Diamond 2 oz Ink Co.	Ink	2 1/8	Clear
(bottom) PS & W Co. Pat. Dec. 11, 77	Ink	1 3/4	Clear
Plain	Ink	2 1/2	Clear

	BOTTOM		
Plain	Unbrella Ink	2 3/4	Cobalt
Plain	Unbrella Ink	2 1/2	Amber
(label) Sanford's Premium Writing Fluid	Ink	2 1/4 x 2	Aqua

EMBOSSING	TYPE	SIZE	COLOR
Plain	Ink	2 1/2	Dark Amber
Plain	Ink	2 3/4	Cobalt
Plain	Ink (sample)	2	Clear

MIDDLE

(bottom) Sanford's Inks	Ink	2 3/4	Aqua
Plain	Ink	2 1/2	Clear
Plain	Ink	2	Clear

BOTTOM

Plain	Cone Ink	2 1/2	Amethyst
(bottom) Carter's 1897 made in U.S.A.	Cone Ink	2 1/2	Honey Amber
Plain	Cone Ink	2 1/2	Emerald

CARBOLINE

The GREAT Petroleum HAIR RESTORER

Of the many hair restorers which, in the last decade, have been brought into the market, only

CARBOLINE

remains. All the others have had their brief day, and are not.

What more is necessary to show that Carboline is a meritorious preparation.

CARBOLINE will restore hair on bald heads.

CARBOLINE will prevent the hair from falling out.

CARBOLINE is an elegant hair dressing.

Wholesale of LANGLEY & MICHAELS CO.,
SAN FRANCISCO, CAL.

SEVEN SEALS, or GOLDEN WONDER.

What's in a name? Nothing but a mark of identification. But if you ask one of the many thousands of Pacific Coast people who have used it, "What's in Seven Seals?" the response will be: "A sure and instantaneous cure for any ache or pain, a prompt remover of Cramps, Diarrhœa, Flux or Cholera Morbus; a mighty foe to Rheumatism."

NO HOUSE SHOULD BE WITHOUT IT.

It has proved a blessing in cases of sudden attack, and by its prompt action has saved many lives and warded off illnesses which, but for its aid, would have been long and severe.

PRICE 50 Cents and $1.00 a Bottle.

Wholesale of LANGLEY & MICHAELS CO., San Francisco, Cal.

KENNEDY & CO, 114 Wood Street, Pittsburg, Penn.

BATCHELOR'S ✳ CELEBRATED ✳ HAIR ✳ DYE.

ESTABLISHED 1831.

Best in the world. Harmless! Reliable! Instantaneous! No disappointment, no ridiculous tints. Remedies the ill effects of bad eyes; leaves the hair soft and beautiful. Black or Brown. Explanatory circulars sent postpaid in sealed envelopes on application, mentioning this catalogue. Sold by all druggists. Applied by experts at

BATCHELOR'S WIG FACTORY,

30 East 10th St., New York City.

GROCERS WILL DO WELL TO CARRY A STOCK OF THE ABOVE GOODS.

O^{RDER}_{FROM} LANGLEY & MICHAELS CO.

☞ SIGNS AND ADVERTISING MATTER SUPPLIED TO THE TRADE ON APPLICATION. ☜

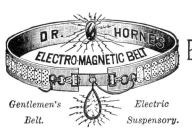

Gentlemen's Belt.   *Electric Suspensory.*

DR. HORNE'S
ELECTRO-MAGNETIC BELT.

BEST SCIENTIFIC MEDICAL BELTS

This Electric Belt will cure the following Diseases without Medicine:

Pains in the Back, Hips, Head or Limbs, Nervous Debility, Lumbago, General Debility, Rheumatism, Paralysis, Neuralgia, Sciatica, Disease of Kidneys, Spinal Diseases, Torpid Liver, Gout, Exhaustion, Emissions, Asthma, Heart Disease, Dyspepsia, Constipation, Erysipelas, Indigestion, Weakness, Impotency, Catarrh, Piles, Epilepsy, Dumb Ague, Diabetes, Hydrocele, etc.

Belts forwarded to any part of the United States, at my expense, on Receipts of Price.

Electro-Magnetic Belts, new style $10.00
Electro-Magnetic Belts, full power 15.00
Electro-Magnetic Belts, 9 improvements 20.00
Electro-Magnetic Trusses 10.00

Dr. W. J. HORNE,
Inventor, Proprietor and Manufacturer

OFFICES: { 191 Wabash Ave., Chicago.
{ 997 Market St., San Francisco,

LADIES' BELT.

RUPTURE
—— Cured by Using ——

DR. HORNE'S ELECTRIC TRUSS.
E. J. IMHAUS, 997 Market Street, S. F.,

HORLICK'S FOOD

NOT FARINACEOUS.   ENTIRELY SOLUBLE.

The Best and Cheapest Food for Infants and Children.

NO OTHER FOOD GIVES SUCH UNIVERSAL SATISFACTION

At the Meeting of the Pædological Society held in Indianapolis, in June, 1882, this Food was unanimously pronounced better than all others. (See Report.)

HORLICK'S DRY EXTRACT OF MALT

PURE   AND   CONVENIENT.

SOLUBLE IN MILK OR WATER.

SUPERIOR TO ALL LIQUID EXTRACTS.

HORLICK'S FOOD CO., RACINE, WIS.

MALTED MILK

Approaches Mother's Milk nearer than any other Milk Preparation yet introduced.

Requires No Cooking, or Addition of Milk.

DISSOLVES IN WATER.   FREE FROM STARCH.

ADDRESS,

MALTED MILK CO.,

RACINE,   WIS.

HIRES' IMPROVED
ROOT BEER PACKAGES

This preparation has steadily grown in public favor during the past ten years, until to-day it is used in every part of the United States and Canada, and a portion of the Old World.

The tons of roots, barks and berries, which are collected in the season of their full development, that enter annually the composition of HIRES' IMPROVED ROOT BEER, have alone, by their intrinsic value, given it national distinction and fame. Therefore, in offering it to the trade, we do so confident that its superior excellency will commend it to your customers, as the best selling and most satisfactory article of the kind ever sold.

WHOLESALE PRICE LIST.

Packages in Dry form................$ 1.75 per dozen.
    "   "   "   .... 18.00 " gross.
    "   " Liquid form......... .... 1.75 " dozen.
    "   "   "   "   .... 20.00 " gross.

CONCENTRATED SOLUTION FOR DRAWING FROM SODA FOUNTAIN.

In Pint Bottles..........75 cents each; $8.50 per dozen.
" One Gallon Cans................. 5.00 " gallon.
" Five   "   "   .... 4.50 " "

If you want the most profitable trade with your fountain or bottling business, manufacture and run HIRES' IMPROVED ROOT BEER

Comic and attractive show cards.

It can be made into a syrup, and run in a soda fountain; it pays and takes better than soda water and all other drinks combined. TRY IT.

We solicit your trade, and shall be pleased to extend you any courtesies we can to further your interests. Hoping to hear from you, I am,

Yours, very trnly,

CHARLES E. HIRES,

PHILADELPHIA, PENN.

Messrs. MARSHALL & SIMMONS, Downington, Penn., write: "We have been selling your Root Beer Packages for years. We also use it in our families and can recommend it to be just what you say about it."

RANSOM & CO., Corry, Penn., says: "It is the best drink ever sold. Every lady thinks it splendid. We make fifty gallons at a time."

THE GENUINE AND ONLY IMPORTED

JOHANN HOFF'S MALT EXTRACT

Introduced into the United States by LEOPOLD HOFF in.............. **1866**
And sold from Hoff's Malt Extract Depot, 542 Broadway, N. Y., Leopold
Hoff Proprietor.

Agency transferred to JOSEPH S. PEDERSEN in...................... **1868**
Depot 2½ Murray Street, N. Y.

TARRANT & COMPANY, SOLE AGENTS in 1869

278, 280 and 282 GREENWICH STREET. New York.

—— THE ——

FIRST - MALT - EXTRACT

Introduced to the Medical Profession, and
after TWENTY-TWO YEARS is still

—— THE ——

Standard Nutritive Tonic

—— FOR ——

Nursing Women Convalescents, the Aged,
Nervous or Dyspeptic.

WARNING.

Druggists are particularly cautioned against a DOMESTIC PREPARATION which is being
foisted upon the trade as a Genuine Imported Johann Hoff's Malt Extract. The article in
question is manufactured in Philadelphia, Penn., and is put up in Squatty Bottle, with cork
covered with yellow wax, giving the package a German appearance.

THE GENUINE AND ONLY IMPORTED

JOHANN HOFF'S MALT EXTRACT,

received by us monthly per steamer of the Hamburg-American Packet Co., and for which we
have been sole agents since 1869, is INVARIABLY put up in bottles as per cut, (especially
adopted for this market in 1868), and is guaranteed Genuine and imported by the signature of
Tarrant & Company on metallic cap, to counterfeit which is felony.

To prevent substitution, Druggists are requested to specify Hoff's Malt Extract,
TARRANT'S when ordering.

Swift's Specific

NATURE'S OWN ANTIDOTE for all Blood Poisons. Sovereign Remedy for *all Skin Diseases*.

NO MERCURY OR POTASH, or any other Mineral Poison.

S. S. S. is made of the roots and herbs gathered in the woods of Georgia.

IT IS AN INFALLIABLE REMEDY FOR

RHEUMATISM, SCROFULA, CONTAGIOUS BLOOD POISON, CANCER, ECZEMA, ULCERS, HEREDITARY BLOOD TAINT, MERCURIAL and VEGETABLE POISON, CATARRH, and for ALL DISEASES of the SKIN.

Beware of Imitations and Counterfeits.

It is unnecessary to speak of the wonderful hold which S. S. S. has upon the confidence he American people as the unrivaled boon for all who suffer from diseases of the blood and n. The thousands of testimonials of remarkable cures effected, on file in the home office the company in this city, which are daily augmented by scores of letters received from al. ts of the United States, is undisputable proof of this.

Books on "Contagious Blood Poison" and on "Skin Diseases" mailed free. For sale all Druggists.

THE SWIFT SPECIFIC CO.,

Drawer 3, Atlanta, Georgia   New York Office, 756 Broadway.

POND'S ✳ EXTRACT.

This is the Genuine

Sold only in bottles with buff wrappers. Our Trade-mark around every bottle. In sickness every drop is worth its weight in gold.

Caution.—*Common law perfectly protects Trade-marks. Persons selling any other preparation, representing that it is* **Pond's Extract,** *or the same as* **Pond's Extract,** *render themselves liable to fine and imprisonment.*

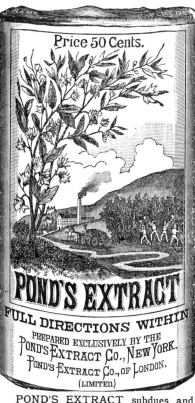

Price 50 Cents.

POND'S EXTRACT

FULL DIRECTIONS WITHIN

PREPARED EXCLUSIVELY BY THE
POND'S EXTRACT CO., NEW YORK.
POND'S EXTRACT CO., OF LONDON.
(LIMITED.)

PRICE LIST.

			Dozen.	Gross.
Pond's Extract, Small			$4 00	$45 00
"	"	Medium	8 00	90 00
"	"	Large	16 00	180 00
"	"	Toilet Cream	8 00	90 00
"	"	Dentifrice	4 00	45 00
"	"	Lip Salve	2 00	20 00
"	"	Toilet Soap doz. bxs.	4 00	45 00
"	"	Ointment	4 00	45 00
"	"	Porous Plaster	1 20	12 00
"	"	Catarrh Remedy	6 00	65 00
"	"	Nasal Syringe	2 00	22 00
"	"	Inhaler, glass	4 00	45 00
"	"	" rubber	8 00	90 00
"	"	Medicated Paper, case 100 packages		12 00

POND'S EXTRACT subdues and heals all kinds of Inflammation, Piles Blind, Bleeding or Itching) Ulcers, Old or New Wounds, Burns, Bruises, Toothache, Earache, Sore Eyes, Scalds, Sprains, Catarrh, Colds, Diarrhœa, Rheumatism, Neuralgia, Diphtheria, Sore Throat, etc.

POND'S EXTRACT is called the WONDER OF HEALING. Used internally and externally. It is unsafe to use any other but the GENUINE with our directions.

Pond's Extract Co., 76 Fifth Avenue, New York.

INTERESTING ITEMS

Left to Right
1. General Taylor Flask 2. Union Flask 3. Cornucopia Flask 4. Expanded Diamond Bottle (Early Clevenger) 5. Leather covered Flask with Ground Top

Left to Right
1. Vase 2. Perfume bottle 3. Fraternal Flask 4. Barrel 5. Cathedral Bulk Ink

Left to Right
1. Liquor 2. Liquor 3. Pharmaceutical 4. Liquor 5. Wooden Canteen
6. Wooden Ships Bottle

Left to Right
1. Harden Hand Grenade 2. Liquor 3. Champagne 4. Horse Shoe Bottle

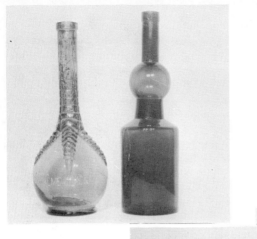

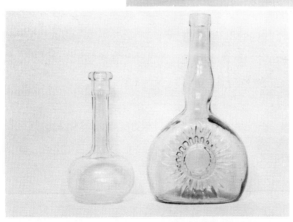

Left to Right
1. Claw Bottle 2. Liquor 3. Hand Grenade 4. Liquor
5. Smoking Bottle 6. Sauce Bottle 7. Unknown

-148-

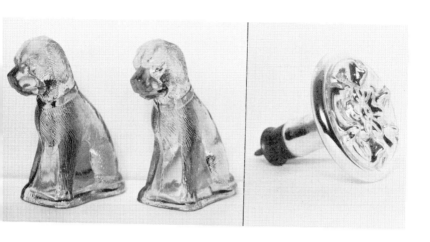

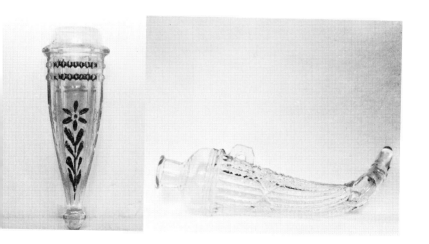

Left to Right
1. (amethyst) Dogs 2. Mirror Stop 3. Car Vase 4. Powder Horn

Top to Bottom
1. Chinese Wares 2. Sock Darner 3. Breast Pump

Top to Bottom
1. Foot Warmer 2. Foot Warmer 3. Molasses Jug 4. Preserve Jar

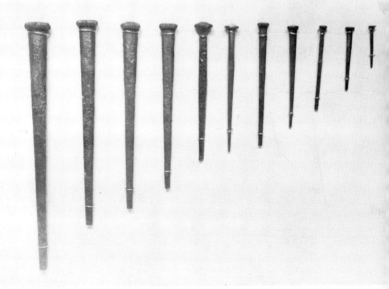

Top to Bottom
1. Mammoth Tooth (10,000 years old). This 8 lb. tooth is but one of the four teeth used by the Mammoth, and was found by the Author near a trading site built by John Jacob Astor in 1811.

2. Square Nail Series.

ARTISTIC COOKERY

Sheeps' Tongues, a la Dominicaine.

This entree suits better for a supper, or rather for a ball-buffet, than for a dinner; however, it can always be admitted in a dinner, if preceded or followed by cold entrees of another kind.

The sheeps' tongues must be salted a l'ecarlate, cooked, well trimmed, and well glazed; they are dished on a jellyborder. The tongues do not rest on the border, the latter having its cavity filled with a circle of wood, on the center of which is fixed a support, that is masked with butter, or paper. The round, and the support, are covered over with salad, composed vegetables, cut into the form of small dice, and mixed with some mayonnaise, prepared with aspic jelly. On the top of the support is fixed a small cup of fat, the base ofwhich is sunk into a thick string of chopped aspic-jelly. A sauce-boatful of egg-mayonnaise, is sent up with this entree.

Ham "Historie"

The sucking-pig represented in the plate, which in reality is not a sucking-pig, but only has the form of one, is in modeled butter; it is only on the back, that the ham is placed. To shape the latter neatly, it should first be entirely boned, wrapped round with a napkin, and so cooked; when done, it is taken out of the napkin to be wrapped up again, and left to cool in the required form; when trimmed and neatly carved, the small animal, which must bear it, should be carved. The piece is surrounded with pretty plaited paper-cases, garnished with glazed truffles; the base of the "pain-vert" is surrounded with bold croutons of aspic-jelly, and indispensable garnish to cold pieces.

Filets of Snipes in Cases

Small cases of folded paper may be purchased everywhere, either of round or oval shape. Paper cases must be oiled previously to be garnished; if their garnish consists of moist materials, the cases can be double. To prepare this dish, the filets of seven or eight snipes must be removed, trimmed, and placed in a "sauté" pan to be cooked with clarified butter. A purrée is prepared with cooked legs of snipes, a few poultry livers, a small part of the giblets of game, some boiled rice, a little sauce, and a piece of butter. The filets are cooked just before sending to table; the purée is warmed without ebullition, and the cases filled up with the latter. On the pureé, a filet of a snipe is placed, then masked immediately with a little good brown sauce, reduced with the perfume of game. The cases are ranged on a baking-sheet, to be kept a few minutes at the mouth of the oven, in order to give brilliance to the sauce covering the filets. The cases are afterward dished up on a folded napkin.

BEVERAGES

Rasberry Shrub

Place red raspberries in a stone jar, cover them with good cider vinegar and let stand over night. In the morning strain, and to each pint of juice, add one pint of sugar; boil for five minutes, skim, and let cool; then bottle and cork tightly.

Egg Wine

One egg, one tablespoonful and one-half glass of cold water, one glass of sherry, sugar, and grated nutmeg to taste. Beat the egg, mixing with it a tablespoonful of cold water; make the wine and water hot, but not boiling; pour on it the egg, stirring all the time. Add sufficient lump sugar to sweeten the mixture, and a little grated nutmeg; put all into a very clean saucepan, set it on a gentle fire, and stir the contents one way until they thicken, but do not allow them to boil. Serve in a glass with sippets of toasted bread or plain crisp biscuits. When the egg is not warmed the mixture will be found easier of digestion, but it is not so pleasant a drink.

To Make Essence of Coffee

To every 1/4 lb. of ground coffee allow 1 small teaspoonful of powdered chicory, 3 small teacupfuls, or 1 pint of water. Let the coffee be freshly ground, and if possible, freshly roasted; put it into a percolator, or filter, with the chicory, and pour slowly over it the above proportion of boiling water. When it has all filtered through, warm the coffee sufficiently to bring it to the simmering point, but do not allow it to boil; then filter it a second time, put it into a clean and dry bottle, cork it well, and it will remain good for several days. Two Tablespoonfuls of this essence are quite sufficient for a breakfastcupful of hot milk. This essence will be found particularly useful to those persons who have to rise extremely early; and having only the milk to make boiling, it is very easily and quickly prepared. When the essence is bottled, pour another 3 teacupfuls of boiling water slowly on the grounds, which, when filtered through, will be a very weak coffee. The next time there is essence to be prepared, make this weak coffee boiling, and pour it on the ground coffee instead of plain water; by this means a better coffee will be obtained. Never throw away the grounds without having made use of them in this manner; and always cork the bottle well that contains this preparation, until the day that it is wanted for making the fresh essence. Prepared coffee essence can now be bought at a reasonable price, and of good quality. It needs to be mixed with boiling water or milk, to be filtered once, then brought to the boiling point, and allow 2 tablespoonfuls for a breakfastcupful of hot milk.

THE CARE OF THE PERSON

Freckles No. 1

Take grated horseradish and put in very sour milk. Let it stand four hours, then wash the face night and morning.

Freckles No. 2

Rectified spirits of wine, one ounce; water, eight ounces; half an ounce of orange-flower water, or one ounce of rosewater; diluted muriatic acid, one teaspoonful; mix. To be used after washing.

Freckles No. 3

Take one ounce lemon juice, one fourth drachm of powdered borax, half drachm sugar. Mix and let them stand in a glass bottle for a few days. Then rub it on the face and hands night and morning. Two teaspoonfuls of lemon juice equal an ounce.

Freckles No. 4

Take of sulpho carbolate of zinc, 2 drachms; glycerine, 3 fluid ounces; alcohol, half a fluid oz.; rose water, enough to make 8 fluid ounces. Apply locally.

To Soften the Hands

To soften the hands, fill a wash-basin half full of fine white sand and soapsuds as hot as can be borne. Wash the hands in this, five minutes at a time, washing and rubbing them in the sand. The best is the flint sand, or the white, powdered quartz sold for filters. It may be used repeatedly by pouring the water away after each washing, and adding fresh to keep it from blowing about. Rinse in warm lather of fine soap, and, after drying, rub them with dry bran or cornmeal. Dust them, and finish with rubbing cold cream well into the skin. This effectrally removes the roughness caused by homework, and should be used every day, first removing ink or vegetables stains with acid.

To Soften the Hands, No. 2

Keep a dish of Indian meal on the toilet stand near the soap, and rub the meal freely on the hands after soaping them for washing. It will surprise you, if you have not tried it, to find how it will cleanse and soften the skin, and prevent chapping.

To Soften the Hands, No. 3

Before retiring take a large pair of gloves and spread mutton tallow inside, also all over the hands. Wear the gloves all night, and wash the hands with olive oil and white castile coap the next morning.

After cleansing the hands with soap, rub them well with oatmeal while still wet. Honey is also very good, used in the same way as lemon juice, well rubbed in at night.

THE FAMILY DOCTOR

Influenza or "Grippe"

It is reported as having been quite fatal in France in 1311 and 1403. In 1570 i also prevailed, and in 1557 spread over Europe, and extended to America. It oc cured again in 1729, 1743, 1775, 1782, 1833, 1837, with notable violence. I the United States, one of the most remarkable epidemics for extent, was that o 1843. Another was that of 1872, following nearly the course of the epizootic a mong horses of the latter part of that year. The last epidemic (1890) has been a re markable one for its extend, invading all Europe and the United States. Mild case require housing and little more. The following prescription will be found excellen† Take of antipyrin, eighteen grains; Dover's powder, twelve grains; powdered ex tract valerian, three grains; mix, and divide into six capsules. Take one every tw hours. If there be a tight cough, take the following: Take of muriate of ammonia thirty grains, deodorized tincture of opium, one drachm; syrup of senega snakeroot one-half ounce; distilled water, one ounce; syrup of balsam tolu, enough to mak three fluid ounces; mix and take a teaspoonful every two hours. Great prostration especially in old people, may call for support by quinine and stimulants, as ho whiskey punches.

---

[1] Jennie A. Hansey, Dr. N.T. Oliver, The Century Cook Book, Dr. N.T. Oliver Treasured Secrets. (1894)

FIGURAL BOTTLES

Left to Right
1. Fish 2. Snake 3. Hand With Gun 4. Cat 5. Cat 6. Dog

Left to Right
1. Poland Water Bottle 2. Russian Black Bear 3. Three Faces 4. Boy with Clo⟨
5. Poodle 6. Madonna 7. Flapper 8. Carrie Nation

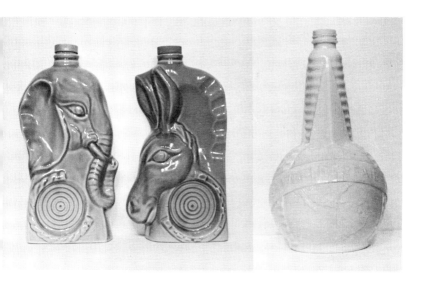

Left to Right

1. Jim Beam Pheasant 2. Jim Beam Fox 3. Jim Beam Political Bottles 4. 1939 Worlds Fair

Left to Right
1. Jim Beam Alaska 2. Jim Beam Hawaii 3. Jim Beam Civil War 4. Jim Beam Civil War

eft to Right
. Jim Beam Wyoming 2. Jim Beam Idaho 3. Jim Beam Montana 4. Jim Beam
Nevada

Left to Right
1. Jim Beam St. Louis 2. Jim Beam Worlds Fair 64-65 3. Jim Beam World Fai
Seattle 4. Jim Beam Oregon

Glafs Reproductions

⊄ During the archaeological Excavations at *Williamfburg*, many Fragments of Eighteenth Century Glass were found.

⊄ To further the Educational Program of *Colonial Williamsburg*, Reproductions in Glassware have been made from original Examples in the restored Buildings and from the excavated Fragments. These have been made available to the Public by *Williamsburg Restoration, Incorporated* through its *Reproductions Program.*

⊄ All the Glassware Reproductions are blown by the ancient *Off-Hand* Process and are hand-formed by Means of Wooden Paddles. Every Piece has its individual Characteristics, as do all Pieces of old Glass, the forming of which depends upon the Skill and Mood of the Artisan.

® identifies registered trademarks owned by Williamsburg Restoration, Inc.

HISTORY OF
BLENKO GLASS CO., INC.

The company's name comes from William Blenko, a British glassmaker who shipped glass to American stained glass studios. In 1893 he came to this country and started a glassmaking business in Kokomo, Indiana, because of the natural gas available there.

Glass was made exclusively for church windows and related uses. He found that the studios were prejudiced against domestic glass, and demanded the imported product. Blenko had to return to England in 1904 where he produced the identical glass, but was now able to sell it in America.

In 1909 he made an attempt in Point Marion, Pennsylvania, and 1913 in Clarksburg West Virginia, using British glassworkers. Both of these efforts failed.

In 1922 Blenko was seventy, but he began a new effort in Milton, West Virginia. His son, William H. Blenko, joined him the following year, and for seven years they struggled in a business which seemed to hold no future.

At this point during the height of the depression, William H. Blenko could see the necessity of producing some other product. He made an arrangement with a large department store in Boston to make handmade flower vases and tableware. This ware was being imported from Venice and instead of the restricted field of making glass for church windows, the company found opened to it a new, wider, and highly promising field.

William Blenko died in 1934, but he had lived to see the tide change. Since then, with the imaginative leadership of William H. Blenko, the fame of Blenko glass has spread far and wide. The decorative accessories and the beautiful stained glass windows utilizing Blenko glass are known all over America. Much of the glass in the windows of Washington Cathedral, the Cathedrals of St. John the Divine and St. Patrick in New York City, the Harkness Library at Yale, the Chapel of Duke University, the Cathedral at Monterrey, Mexico, and the Air Force Academy Chapel, is Blenko.

In 1937 Blenko became associated with the restoration work at Colonial Williamsburg and has been the licensed manufacturer of all their glass reproductions for over 20 years.

At the beginning there were two Swedish glassworkers who were highly experienced in such work. Three of four men who learned from them are still on the job, and are now teaching others. Now, interested young men in the community have an opportunity to learn a fine skill. Most of the craftsmen are young, in the late thirties and under, on the average. There is ample opportunity for practice, essential in a skill like glassblowing, which is more a personal art than a mechanical process. The truly interested boys practice on their own time, learning and improving as they go along. The disinterested quickly fall out of the ranks. The older experienced workers willingly lend tools and advice, the younger men, as they master the trade, find continual opportunity in the general expanding of the company's business.

*Williamsburg Restoration Glass

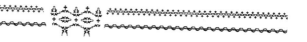

REPRODUCTIONS

Reproduction Glassware plays a very important part in the hobby of bottle col-
cting. The average collector realizes that it would be unlikely that he or she
ould find or obtain very many of the original historical types of bottles. Also, if
e various types of originals are to be purchased, the price would be out of range
most pocket books. It is with this thought that the Nuline, Blenko, and the
evenger Glass Works are reproducing the originals and offering their glasswares
the public at prices within the range of every collector.

This type of glass line may be looked upon as a sound investment for the future.
rlier reproductions, made by these same companies years ago, are presently com-
nding a greater price than their original value.

Like all products that are offered to the general public and that resemble an
rlier product, there always will be those people, who will take advantage of the
llector by offering him reproductions as originals. It must be understood that the
mpanies making reproduction glass do not condone and least of all wish to see this
e of practice. Their sincere feelings are filled with pride, honor and craftsman-
p.

The best protection for the collector is to become better acquainted, and in-
ase his knowledge of reproduction products. It is with this in mind that various
es are shown on the succeeding pages to acquaint the collector with the types
d styles, with their history, that are being offered today.

HISTORY OF
WHEATON GLASS COMPANY
(Nuline Products)

The Wheaton name has been associated with glass making since the T. C. Wheaton Company was established in 1888 and the enterprise grew rapidly and became a world wide enterprise of twenty-eight related firms all under the direct management and control of the current president, Mr. Frank H. Wheaton, Jr.

During the first half century of its well ordered growth the company produced hand made items of blown and pressed glassware. The years since 1938 have witnessed more spectacular growth, coupled with the installation of automatic production equipment, diversification of activities to include several plastic factories, and the extension of the Wheaton services to the world at large.

The principal products of the Wheaton Companies are molded items of glass and plastic, particularly containers, closures and related items pertaining to the field of packaging. One prominent feature in the Wheaton Company growth is its research and specialized engineering service to the glass and plastic industries where in glass and plastics are combined in an interesting and revolutionary manner.

Handmade bottles for the "antique" and pharmaceutical trade were original items in the small handblown shops under the founder, Theodore Corson Wheaton, Ph. D., M.D., founder of the T. C. Wheaton Company who died in 1931. The presidency of the firm passed to Frank Hayes Wheaton and in 1938 to Frank Hayes Wheaton, Jr. The firm is still completely owned by the Wheaton family and its founders' decendents. Its products now include the most sophisticated containers for the cosmetic and pharmaceutical industries but a small hand shop is maintained in its modern factory producing some of the original items in the oldest traditions of handblown glass making.

Because of the resurgence of public interest in "antique" bottles, the firm recently has begun the automatic production of many of its oldest handmade "antique" bottles for the consumer trade throughout the country and the world.

1888

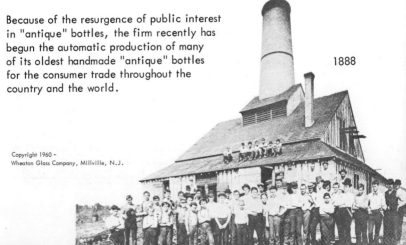

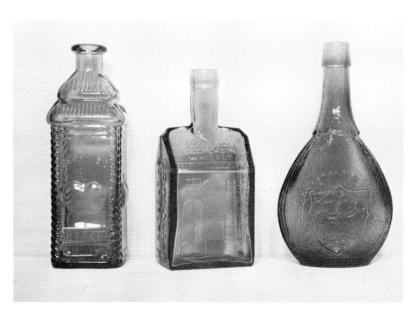

Berrings Apple Bitters	Cabin Bitters Bottle	Masonic Union Bottle
Rogers Bros. Seal Bottle	Washington Portrait Bottle	Continental Pinched Bottle

HISTORY OF THE
CLEVENGER GLASS WORKS

Established in early 1900, the Clevenger Bro's Glass Works in Clayton, New Jersey has been producing glassware that became famous throughout the nation. The former owner, William (Allie) Clevenger (now deceased), was one of the finest glass blowers in the New Jersey region. By the use of the off hand method he produced pitchers and vases that are highly prized by collectors throughout the United States.

In 1950 Allie Clevenger married Mrs. Myrtle Whildon. Her first husband Ron Whildon, had at one time owned four pieces of Stoddard glass, originally made in Sandwich, Massachusetts. However, before he sold the original molds to a man from New York for a sum of $4,800 he had new molds made from the originals. After the death of Mr. Whildon the molds passed on to Mrs. Clevenger, formerly Mrs. Whildon. Mr. and Mrs. Clevenger then began to collect other molds to add to their growing collection. The molds that were acquired were not the original molds but exact copies from the original bottles, right down to the flaws in the original wooden molds of the famous old South Jersey glass.

With only 15 employees the little glass factory in Clayton, New Jersey began to place their wares on the market. They have produced such famous bottles as the Booz and Jenny Lind. One of the most popular is the Jenny Lind bottle. During the early days when commemorative bottles became popular, a glass manufacturer, in Fislerville, New Jersey, cut a Jenny Lind mold which bears the name Fislerville on it. This name is of special interest, because in 1850 Fislerville was the name of the town of Clayton, where the Clevenger plant stills blows this flask.

Altogether the Clevenger Glass Works owns 70 molds of which they are presently producing 63. Some of the molds cost over a thousand dollars to make. The collection of molds were acquired by the purchase of old bottles from which new molds were made. These molds were cut in wood first, from them brass or iron molds were cast and those in turn were engraved to make them perfect.

The employees at the Clevenger plant are second and fourth generation glass workers who learned their trade early in life, mostly in the South Jersey glass factories which have since gone out of business. The methods used are 18th century. Production is from about the middle of October to February. They work completely through one color before going to the next, beginning with amber on through green, blue and amethyst.

In 1960 Allie Clevenger passed away. Some time later Myrtle Clevenger, wife of the deceased, married William Stout Bowers, the former manager of the plant. Together they kept the small plant operating until 1966 when due to the deaths of some of the older employees the factory was closed down after 62 years in business. It appeared to be the end of this famous glass line. This shocked many lovers of fine glass. The day was saved when a Mr. James Elwood Travis of Millville, New Jersey purchased the factory which includes the company name, molds and all other equipment. He operates a small factory in Vineland, New Jersey, which produces paper weights, vases, fancy pitchers and other glass pieces. The new owner placed the company back into production and plans to produce all the molds that the Clevengers had acquired over the years. He will also, produce the glass in the same old South Jersey tradition the plant has always followed.

Chubby Creamer	George Washington	Small Footed Creamer
Squat Creamer	Stoddard Vase	Stars & Shields

Albany
Glass Works

Jenny
Lind

General
Mac Arthur

Old Fashioned
Diamond

Stoddard
Decanter

Hobnail

My
Country

Eagle &
Grape

Scroll

Washington
& Taylor

E.G. Booz

Railroad

Elephant   Violin   Crown

Moon &   Stoddard   Daisy
Star   Pitcher

Sunflower   Decanter   Doughnut
                   Vase

        Button &   Cantaloupe   Diamond
        Daisy

-Y-

-Z-

For other books on bottle collecting,
write for free illustrative brochure.

OLD TIME BOTTLE PUBLISHING COMPANY
Department L   Phone:
611 Lancaster Dr. NE   Area Code 503
Salem, Oregon 97301   362-1446

3455